Prepare for the Great Tribulation and the Era of Peace

Prepare for the Great Tribulation and the Era of Peace

Volume XIV:
January 1, 1999 – March 31, 1999

by John Leary

PUBLISHING COMPANY
P.O. Box 220 • Goleta, CA 93116
(800) 647-9882 • (805) 692-0043 • Fax: (805) 967-5843

The publisher recognizes and accepts that the final authority regarding these apparitions and messages rests with the Holy See of Rome, to whose judgement we willingly submit.

– The Publisher

Cover art by Josyp Terelya

Library of Congress Number # 95-73237

Published by:
Queenship Publishing
P.O. Box 220
Goleta, CA 93116
(800) 647-9882 • (805) 692-0043 • Fax: (805) 957-5843

Printed in the United States of America

ISBN: 1-57918-115-5

Acknowledgments

It is in a spirit of deep gratitude that I would like to acknowledge first the Holy Trinity: Father, Jesus, and the Holy Spirit, the Blessed Virgin Mary and the many saints and angels who have made this book possible.

My wife, Carol, has been an invaluable partner. Her complete support of faith and prayers has allowed us to work as a team. This was especially true in the many hours of indexing and proofing of the manuscript. All of our family has been a source of care and support.

I am greatly indebted to Josyp Terelya for his very gracious offer to provide the art work for this publication. He has spent three months of work and prayer to provide us with a selection of many original pictures. He wanted very much to enhance the visions and messages with these beautiful and provocative works. You will experience some of them throughout these volumes.

A very special thank you goes to my spiritual director, Fr. Leo J. Klem, C.S.B. No matter what hour I called him, he was always there with his confident wisdom, guidance and discernment. His love, humility, deep faith and trust are a true inspiration.

My appreciation also goes to Father John V. Rosse, my good pastor who is retiring from Holy Name of Jesus Church. He has been open, loving and supportive from the very beginning.

There are many friends and relatives whose interest, love and prayerful support have been a real gift from God. Our own Wednesday, Monday and First Saturday prayer groups deserve a special thank you for their loyalty and faithfulness.

Finally, I would like to thank Bob and Claire Schaefer of Queenship Publishing for providing the opportunity to bring this message of preparation, love and warnings to you the people of God.

John Leary, Jr.

Dedication

To the Most Holy Trinity

God

The Father, Son and Holy Spirit

The Source of

All

Life, Love and Wisdom

Publisher's Foreword

John has, with some exceptions, been having visions twice a day since they began in July, 1993. The first vision of the day usually takes place during morning Mass, immediately after he receives the Eucharist. If the name of the church is not mentioned, it is a local Rochester, NY, church. When out of town, the church name is included in the text. The second vision occurs in the evening, either at Perpetual Adoration or at the prayer group that is held at Holy Name of Jesus Church.

Various names appear in the text. Most of the time, the names appear only once or twice. Their identity is not important to the message and their reason for being in the text is evident. First names have been used, when requested by the individual.

We are grateful to Josyp Terelya for the cover art, as well as for the art throughout the book. Josyp is a well-known visionary and also, the author of *Witness* and most recently *In the Kingdom of the Spirit.*

This volume covers messages from January 1, 1999 through March 31, 1999. The volumes have been coming out quarterly due to the urgency of the messages.

Volume I: July, 1993 through June, 1994.
Volume II: July, 1994 through June, 1995.
Volume III: July, 1995 through July 10, 1996.
Volume IV: July 11, 1996 through September 30, 1996.
Volume V: October 1, 1996 through December 31, 1996.
Volume VI: January 1, 1997 through March 31, 1997.
Volume VII: April 1, 1997 through June 30, 1997.
Volume VIII: July 1, 1997 through September 30, 1997.
Volume IX: October 1, 1997 through December 31, 1997.
Volume X: January 1, 1998 through March 31, 1998.
Volume XI: April 1, 1998 through June 30, 1998.
Volume XII: July 1, 1998 through September 30, 1998.
Volume XIII: October 1, 1998 through December 31, 1998.

The Publisher

Foreword

It was in July of 1993 that Almighty God, especially through Jesus, His Eternal Word, entered the life of John Leary in a most remarkable way. John is 56 years old and is a retired chemist from Eastman Kodak Co., Rochester, New York. He lives in a modest house in the suburbs of Rochester with Carol, his wife of thirty-three years, and Catherine, his youngest daughter. His other two daughters, Jeanette and Donna, are married and have homes of their own. John has been going to daily Mass since he was seventeen and has been conducting a weekly prayer group in his own home for twenty-five years. For a long time, he has been saying fifteen decades of the Rosary each day.

In April of 1993 he and his wife made a pilgrimage to Our Lady's shrine in Medjugorje, Yugoslavia. While there, he felt a special attraction to Jesus in the Blessed Sacrament. There he became aware that the Lord Jesus was asking him to change his way of life and to make Him his first priority. A month later in his home, Our Lord spoke to him and asked if he would give over his will to Him to bring about a very special mission. Without knowing clearly to what he was consenting, John, strong in faith and trust, agreed to all the Lord would ask.

On July 21, 1993 the Lord gave him an inkling of what would be involved in this new calling. He was returning home from Toronto in Canada where he had listened to a talk of Maria Esperanza (a visionary from Betania, Venezuela) and had visited Josyp Terelya. While in bed, he had a mysterious interior vision of a newspaper headline that spelled "DISASTER." Thus began a series of daily and often twice daily interior visions along with messages, mostly from Jesus. Other messages were from God the Father, the Holy Spirit, the Blessed Virgin Mary, his guardian angel and many of the saints, especially St. Therese of Lisieux. These messages he recorded on his word processor. In the beginning, they were quite short, but they became more extensive as the weeks passed by. At the time of this writing, he is still receiving visions and messages.

These daily spiritual experiences, which occur most often immediately following Communion, consist of a brief vision which becomes the basis of the message that follows. They range widely on a great variety of subjects, but one might group them under the following categories: warnings, teachings and love messages. Occasionally, there are personal confirmations of some special requests that he made to the Lord.

The interior visions contain an amazing number of different pictures, some quite startling, which hardly repeat themselves. In regard to the explicit messages that are inspired by each vision, they contain deep insights into the kind of relationship God wishes to establish with His human creatures. There, also, is an awareness of how much He loves us and yearns for our response. As a great saint once wrote: "Love is repaid only by love." On the other hand, God is not a fool to be treated lightly. In fact, did not Jesus once say something about not casting pearls before the swine? Thus, there are certain warnings addressed to those who shrug God off as if He did not exist or is not important in human life.

Along with such warnings, we become more conscious of the reality of Satan and the forces of evil "...which wander through the world seeking the ruin of souls." We used to recite this at the end of each low Mass. In His love and concern for us, Our Lord keeps constantly pointing out how frail we humans are in the face of such evil angelic powers. God is speaking of the necessity of daily prayer, of personal penance, and of turning away from atheistic and material enticements which are so much a part of our modern environment.

Perhaps the most controversial parts of the messages are those which deal with what we commonly call Apocalyptic. Unusual as these may be, in my judgment, they are not basically any different than what we find in the last book of the New Testament or in some of the writings of St. Paul. After a careful and prayerful reading of the hundreds of pages in this book, I have not found anything contrary to the authentic teaching authority of the Roman Catholic Church.

The 16th Century Spanish mystic, St. John of the Cross, gives us sound guidelines for discerning the authenticity of this sort of phenomena involving visions, locutions, etc. According to him, there are three possible sources: the devil, some kind of self-imposed hypnosis or God. I have been John's spiritual confidant for over five years. I have tested him in various spiritual ways and I am most confident that all he has put into these messages is neither of the devil nor of some kind of mental illness. Rather, they are from the God who, in His love for us, wishes to reveal His own Divine mind and heart. He has used John for this. I know that John is quite ready to abide by any decision of proper ecclesiastical authority on what he has written in this book.

— Rev. Leo J. Klem, C.S.B.
Rochester, New York
1993

Note: *As of December, 1998 my spiritual advisor, Father Leo Klem moved to the Basilian Infirmary in Toronto, Ontario, Canada. I am most appreciative to Father for these five years as my spiritual advisor. He has been a source of discernment, love and support. It is with gratitude that I welcome Father Don McCarthy as my new spiritual advisor.*

— John Leary

Dear Reader:

As John's spiritual advisor, I have carefully read Volume XIV and I have found nothing contradicting Catholic faith and morals. Pray for John. His mission is not an easy walk. Yet, he does it prayerfully, humbly, and obediently to God and His Church.

— Fr. Don McCarthy, C.S.B.
May 4, 1999
Rochester, New York

Visions and Messages of John Leary:

Friday, January 1, 1999: (Solemnity of Mary)

After Communion, I could see a young family coming together. Jesus said: ***"My people, as you start the New Year, you have visions of youth and a fresh start. But when you consider that you are really one year older, you see how quickly life passes you by. You have very little time on this earth; for all that you hope to accomplish. Let your spiritual life lead your priorities in what you do. Do not be taken up with visions of making more money in worldly possessions, but keep concentrated on your daily commitment to your love for Me. By keeping your focus on Me, you will be forever young in the glory of My love for you. One day all of these things will come to an end. Rejoice in the thought of being with Me in a youthful glorified body. All of those faithful to My Will will experience this reward with Me in Heaven. Your joy in Heaven will be complete and your life then will be the fulfillment of your dream to see Me in My beatific vision."***

Later, at Adoration, I could see a baby lying in some hay in a manger. Jesus said: ***"My people, look at My humble birth and the little means necessary for living. Those who think they need many possessions to survive are sadly mistaken. A small shelter, a little food and that is all you really need physically. As you look at the hay, it seems very comfortable and has an insulating effect from the cold. It is your priorities of being comfortable today and for many years that some are most concerned about. I tell you to be more concerned about the life of the soul and the threat of the evil one in taking your soul. I will provide for your living in many ways as I feed the sparrows and dress the lilies of the field. You are to take care of your body, but not to necessarily pamper it with your excesses. Fear only the one who can cast you into the flames***

of Hell. My justice will fall on those who are selfish and do not share with their neighbor. But the upright will enjoy an eternity with Me in Heaven. So seek the comfort of your soul in My grace over any bodily comforts that could be quickly taken away."

Saturday, January 2, 1999: (Leo Remacle's memorial Mass 11:00)

After Communion, I could see a long dark tunnel leading to a light. I received a message from Leo as I recognized his voice. Leo said: ***"I want to thank everyone who came to today's Mass and my funeral Mass. I love all of my family very much and I thank you for all of your preparations for the Masses. Especially thank the priests at both services. I could see the light of Jesus and there is nothing to fear of death. Some people require purification, either on earth or in Purgatory. All Jesus asks of you is to love Him and He will bring you to Heaven. I will be praying for all of you and I ask that you continue to pray for me as well."***

Later, at Adoration, I could see a king dressed in velvet purple robes and all the people were around him. Jesus said: ***"My people, as you approach the feast of the Epiphany, look on your King in the manger. The three kings of the Magi knew of the glory of My Presence as they followed My star. They brought Me gifts befitting a king. I am more than a king, you have before you the Son of God who created you. As you go out of your way to make a show of honor for your presidents and kings, prepare to meet Me as one more famous than these. When you heard of the Wisdom of Solomon, you were shaken by his understanding. But you have a greater than Solomon here in Me. You have seen many prophets as Moses, Abraham and Elijah, but you have a greater man of God in Me. Rejoice and give praise and adoration to your Heavenly King. All those who give Me honor and love will be the ones to share your soul's joy in My Presence in Heaven."***

Sunday, January 3, 1999: (Epiphany)

After Communion, I could see a branch clearly but the background was out of focus. Then I saw someone graduating with a cap and gown. Jesus said: ***"My people, I am the vine and you are the branches. Apart from Me you can do nothing. Never lose sight of your goal of one day being with Me in Heaven. Keep***

your eyes on Me and never lose focus of your desire to be with Me. As you celebrate the three kings coming to see Me, remember that one day at your death, you will see your King in all of My glory. Think of your death as a graduation into the next life as you pass from here very quickly. In order for one to graduate, you need to study and pass your courses. Think of life as your courses, and when you have shown love for Me and your neighbor, you will pass the course of life. Prepare now so you can be with Me in Heaven. By your daily prayers and following My Will, you will fight the good fight and win your goal of Heaven. Choose Me over the world and you will share in My eternal life."

Later, at Adoration, I could see some new thick Bibles coming off a printing press line. Jesus said: ***"My people, you have seen the new Bible and Lectionary translations come out. There are some in different quarters that want My Word translated to fit their itching ears. They are not satisfied with the way My inspired Word was given, so they have changed it to fit their fancy. Little by little people in authority are giving way to those with the loudest complaint. Many are still uncomfortable with My Words, because My Will limits their lifestyles. To be a faith-filled person, it requires giving up of your will to Me. It is hard for you to take orders from another, and man wants to control his life. In everything you do, you are faced with an ever increasing evil influence. This evil age will reach its height when the Antichrist will take over. From thereon, evil will be vanquished with My victory over all the powers of the demons. As quickly as the Antichrist will gain worldly control, I will humble him with My comet of chastisement. All evil is about to be cleansed from the earth. Seek My help and do not let evil temptations seduce you. I come to separate the tares and the wheat. Be ever vigilant for My judgment that I will not find you wanting."***

Monday, January 4, 1999:

After Communion, I could see three bright white triangles filled in and they were aligned perfectly over each other in the shape of a triangular prism. Jesus said: ***"My people, I am giving you a unique look and understanding of the mystery of the Trinity. You in your limited knowledge do not have the ability to compre-***

hend God. It is the Three Persons — Father, Son and Holy Spirit — by which We have revealed ourselves to you, but We work as One and are not separate. You know the Three Persons by the different characteristics that have been assigned to each Person, but again We all share these attributes of love, creation and compassion. I came to the earth so I could share in your pain, disappointments and frustrations. My love for all of My creations is so intense that I took on the form of a man and gave My life up for your sins. Even My Incarnation as a man is a mystery for you to understand. I continue that love by making Myself present in the consecrated Host for you. Many of these things you are having to believe by faith now, but when you come to Heaven in your glorified bodies, you will understand more depth in My infinite love in My beatific vision. Treasure all Three Persons in your heart, because we are with you at all times. Give honor and glory to God for all that we share with you. Accept Me into your lives and follow My Will for you, and you will have no fear of what is to come."

Later, I could see an image on a computer screen showing how it was fading away. Jesus said: ***"My people, you have made some advances in your technology, but most of these improvements have been brought about with computers. You have become so comfortable with your devices, that you have failed to understand how vulnerable you are. Since Adam's fall you have been imperfect and many of the things you make are also imperfect. It is not surprising that a simple date will be your undoing. You have grown to depend on yourselves instead of depending on My help. In your present state you do not even realize how depraved you really are. When many of your systems start to fail, you will once again be brought to your knees by your own bad decisions. Unfortunately, there will be a very chaotic time when many of your services will cease being provided. This could be an excellent opportunity for the One World people and the Antichrist to take over your world. They will use this means or war to give their excuse to declare martial law. The final battle with the evil ones is drawing to a close as time for My victory draws near. Have no fear of what tribulation is to come, for I will protect the souls of My faithful. You will be tested dearly in your faith, but with perseverence, you*** *will live to see My new Era of Peace. My coming again in triumph will bring you every joy you have dreamed of."*

Tuesday, January 5, 1999:

After Communion, I could see a Church with an amphitheater shape centered around the altar. Jesus said: ***"My people, you are comfortable in your churches today, but you are witnessing many changes in My Church all over the world. In your area there are certain quarters trying to deal with an artificial shortage of priests. Many churches are about to be closed under the guise of not enough priests. If you encouraged and nurtured vocations, there would be no shortage. These same quarters are changing My interpretation of Scripture to their own hearing. These are the same people that are not in full support of your present pope John Paul II. Pray for him, as by his own admission, he will be leaving soon. Behind the scenes, these evil people will be forcing him to leave, so they can put in their own man as pope. Pray for the faithful not to be swayed in their faith, as the age of apostasy will only worsen. I will soon bring My victory over all of these evil ones, as they will be cast into Hell. My faithful will be protected and brought into My Era of Peace. Have no fear, for I will lead you to a land of milk and honey."***

Later, at Adoration, I could see a dark night in a cemetery with several tombstones. There was a stream of mud which seemed to carry away the evil souls to Hell. Jesus said: ***"My people, look around you to see many people dying at all ages. Even look among your friends and relatives how often there is a death in the family. Your number of years on this earth are very few indeed, and you do not know how long you will be here. Life is very fragile and could end for any number of causes. You should be aware of death, because it is while you are alive, that you can plan for your final destination. Do not be wrapped up so much in this life's activities, that you do not prepare to meet Me at your judgment. I am a God of love and I ask you to let Me be a daily partner in your lives. By listening to My Word and following My ways, you will have eternal life with Me in Heaven. Even if you look foolish to others for giving your life over to Me, you are making the right commitment for your soul in loving and praising Me.***

The joy of living eternally in Heaven far outweighs any earthly joy which passes away in minutes. Think of death only as your transition into the next life, but do not let Satan detour you from coming with Me. He can only offer you hate and eternal suffering in Hell, so do not be taken in by materialism or any worldly fame. Seek to join your heart with Mine forever, by starting that love here on earth. As I have loved you, I ask you to love Me, and your reward will last forever in Heaven."

Wednesday, January 6, 1999:

After Communion, I could see an old bookcase with old dark covered books which after a while disappeared. Jesus said: ***"My people, as you look at these old books of history, they are rarely read and even rewritten with people's agendas. Man has been weak since Adam and has been fighting constant wars through the years. Little has been learned of compromise and peace, only a desire for conquest inspires your leaders. As you fail to learn from your past mistakes, you will be doomed to repeat your wars of greed and conquest. Your spiritual lives are in the same condition as your physical lives. You are weak in sin and you are a sinner, even though you may want to deny it. Again, you repeat your sins, since you have not learned to avoid them. If you make a point with My help to struggle in stopping your sins, it is possible to diminish your sins. It must be a conscious effort to avoid temptations and near occasions of sin to improve. Do not despair in your attempts to remain holy, but always keep trying to follow My Will in all you do."***

Thursday, January 7, 1999:

After Communion, I could see many clergy lined up to a gathering before St. Peter's in Rome. Jesus said: ***"My people, a time is coming soon when My clergy will be gathered together for a special election of the next pope. My pope son, John Paul II, is about to be replaced for reasons of health and age. There will then be two popes reigning at once, as John Paul II will leave Rome. There will be a lot of celebration, but this next pope will be an Antipope, one of the beasts in Revelation. He will be cunning and eventually he will lead people astray as he will accommodate***

the preparation for the coming Antichrist. This event of John Paul II's leaving will bring about a schism in My Church. My remnant will split away from this evil pope into an underground church. This is the sign to go into hiding, as soon they will come to your house demanding everyone to take the Mark of the Beast to buy and sell. For those who refuse to take the chip in the hand or forehead will be taken to detention centers as enemies of the New World Order. If you are in hiding before they come to find you, you will be protected by My angels from imprisonment. They will come to people's houses with Gestapo tactics before martial law is declared. Fear not this time of testing, for I will protect your souls from the evil ones. You may suffer persecution for a brief time, but My victory will soon bring My faithful to My Era of Peace on a renewed earth."

At the prayer group, I could see some gold wedding rings on a tray with many jewels and gold pieces. Jesus said: ***"My people, you are My spouse and I desire you to love Me with all of your heart, mind and soul. These wedding rings represent our love relationship. I have given you free will, because I want you to love Me by your own decision. I do not force you out of duty or threat to love Me. I give My love to you freely and unconditionally. You are the ones to accept Me or reject Me. Do not be taken up with the allurement of riches, but come to Me as your Savior. Those who marry give their love to each other by their own free will and that is how you must come to Me. Those who follow Me will have an eternal reward in Heaven, while those who hate Me will join the demons in a place for the accursed."***

I could see a glow of light on a mountain as a volcano grew more active with smoke and lava. Jesus said: ***"My people, as another sign of the End Times, you will see an increasing amount of volcanic activity which will coincide with an increase in earthquakes. The crust of the earth will be in dishevelment as evil worsens in this age. Seek My protection in your prayers and I will guard your souls."***

I could see in the clouds a baby's picture which gave David a chance to speak. David (my deceased son) said: ***"Thank you for remembering me and seeking my help in your needs. I take all of your petitions before the Lord. I am assisting you in your diffi-***

culties as you have asked. I continue to watch over my family and I share my love with all of you and your families. On this anniversary of my birth, never cease praying to perfect your lives. There is nothing on earth that should distract you from Jesus. Keep faithful to God so you all can greet me in Heaven."

I could see a woman in flowing clothes and St. Elizabeth Ann Seton came and said: ***"My dear children, you are all called by your Baptism to reach out to help your brother and sister in Christ. Follow my example in going the extra mile to lend a helping hand. The children especially need your help both in secular ways, but even more importantly in spiritual ways. It is your responsibility to pass the faith on to the next generations."***

I could see a beautiful garden of flowers and beautiful hedges. There was a glowing light that shone everywhere as you could feel the presence of God. Jesus said: ***"My people, I am giving you a little taste of the Heaven on earth that will come with My renewal in the Era of My Peace. My faithful will be growing in My Divine Will and learning My ceaseless praises. If you are to come to Heaven, you must be perfected in every way. As the angels constantly sing My praises, you will desire to do the same as your love for Me will join you in My one being. Even on your present earth, you can praise Me in adoration of My Blessed Sacrament and you can spend some time meditating on My love in your prayers. See now, My children, that this life is a training ground to prepare you for your entrance into Heaven."***

I could see some bright clouds with many colors and God the Father came forth. God the Father said: ***"'I AM' comes to you to give you a glimpse into Heaven. You are celebrating this year in My honor before John Paul II's announced jubilee. These are serious days of tribulation as your age of apostasy comes to a close. The evil ones will have one last attempt at stealing souls from Heaven. Your faith must be like that of a mustard seed that grows from the smallest of seeds to a large bush. So it is with your faith which is given to you as a gift. You must nourish your faith by giving it the word of My Son, Jesus. He has revealed to you how to live your lives in My witness. Never lose sight of your God. Look for Me in all of creation, since everything is a reflection of My hand's work."***

I could see some waters of a stream as the fresh water flowed into the salt of the ocean. Jesus said: ***"My people, you will read of My Baptism in your readings shortly. Baptism of My grace is a cleansing water that washes away your sins. As you have celebrated My First Coming, so you see Me for the first time when your original sin is forgiven. Renew your own Baptismal vows by renouncing Satan and repenting of your sins. It is this new life with Me that your soul is attracted to. My love and grace are instilled in you for every time you receive one of My sacraments. So, do not belittle Baptism for your infants. They need to be drawn into My Mystical Body as soon as possible, lest they die without My graces."***

Friday, January 8, 1999:

At Holy Rosary Church Adoration, Portland, Oregon, I could see the pillars of the Supreme Court Building. Jesus said: ***"My people, you are witnessing the impeachment trial of your president, but he is being charged for lesser reasons than his other offenses. As many will come later this month to protest the abortions in your country, you have in your president an advocate of abortion both in your country and all over the world. His advocating of killing babies and his open sins of perversion of the flesh are far worse than his lying under oath. It is ironic that he is on trial for lying, when he has done so all of his career. He has not been held accountable, until now, for any of his actions. But just as he has had his day in court, everyone will have their day of accounting at your judgment. You, America, are on trial as well, for your allow these abortions to occur because it is convenient. You are acting in My place by snuffing out the lives of these innocent children. Your country and others are paying a heavy price for the sins of the flesh and abortion. As each year passes, there are more chastisements that are stripping you of your possessions. You were aghast at the killings in the gas chambers of the Jews under Hitler, but where is your sense of guilt for killing millions of My babies each year? Have you no fear of My punishment, or do you not see the severity of your sin? There is coming a moment of My justice, when your nation will be brought low for its crimes. Pray and repent of your sins, while you still***

have time. I am coming soon to separate the evil ones from My faithful. Persevere in your persecution, and I will bring you to the joy of My Era of Peace."

Later, at Holy Rosary, Portland, Oregon, after Communion, I could see a statue of Mary with rays of light shining from her. Mary said: ***"My dear children, I welcome you to this church, for this church loves me and my Son, dearly. They have great devotion and are faithful to my Son in adoring him. They honor me in their Rosaries and prayers. They are united with the heart of my Jesus and my heart as well, since our hearts are as one. Continue to pray for my intentions, especially for stopping abortions. You have seen my days of holding Jesus in my womb come to completion with His birth at Christmas. I pondered all of these events in my heart and I am blessed to be the mother of my God. Come to me with all of your prayer requests and I will bring them to my Son. Have faith that He will answer your prayers in His way and in His time. Thank you for coming to see my Son and for answering my call."***

Saturday, January 9, 1999:

At Holy Rosary, Portland, Oregon, after Communion, I could see a woman going into a pew at church. Jesus said: ***"My people, a good and faithful wife is worth more than any earthly treasure. Your children are like olive plants around your table. Love and admire your wife, so that you may keep the fire alive in your marriage. A wife is your helpmate and with her, you both can walk the narrow road to Heaven. I am there present with both of you through the grace of the Sacrament of Matrimony. Wives should love their husbands as well, for you are both gifts of life to each other. A faithful husband is also to be treasured, so he can guide and protect the family. It is from this family setting that I bring forth new life and you are to honor and respect these gifts of life. Never violate the sacredness of the marriage bond and do everything in your power to preserve this union which I have joined together. I love all of My people and I have set before you the example of My Holy Family, that you may imitate the lives of Mary and St. Joseph. By following My Will and giving good example to your children, your joy will be complete in My love."***

Later, at Holy Rosary, Portland, Oregon, I could see a little window in church looking out into the dark of night. Then a bright light shone in from the window. Jesus said: ***"My people, I am showing you this window as a window to the soul. When you are first born into the world, you inherit the darkness of original sin from Adam. You are all called to receive the Baptism of My grace to cleanse away your sin and bathe you in the glory of My graces. It is My bearing of all of your sins that allows you to rid your original sin. My death has conquered sin and all of its effects. My grace in My sacraments replenishes your soul every time you seek forgiveness of your sins. As a grace of your Baptism, you are made a new member of My Mystical Body. This is also a beginning of your sharing of your grace with others. By your Baptism you are called forth to evangelize others in the faith. The courage and spirit of your love for Me must be passed on to your friends and relatives and especially your children. This is the commitment I ask of all of My followers to do all you can for your neighbor both spiritually and physically."***

Sunday, January 10, 1999: (Baptism of Jesus)

At Holy Rosary, Portland, Oregon, after Communion, I could see the cross of Jesus at the Holy Sepulcher, Jerusalem and my eye focused on the foot of the cross where I dwelled for a time. Jesus said: ***"My people, as you are Baptized into My Church, see yourselves as at the start of your journey to Calvary. One day you are appointed to die and come to Me to make an accounting for your life at your judgment. Some have short lives, while others live into their later years. How ever long you have to live, you are to live it to the fullest for My glory. Be thankful for this opportunity in life to follow My Will and My plan for your life. Each life has beautiful things to accomplish, that only you are given to do. That is why each life is precious in its own right, and should not be denied its right to life. This is true for each life from conception to death. So, you are to take a stand for protecting life at all of its stages. Do not allow the evil one to take the lives of My babies. Pray and do acts of love in protesting your evil laws that accept abortion. The more you help your neighbor, even the defenseless, the more you show your love for Me. Give witness to***

all those around you that you are against abortion and do not be afraid of any criticism on taking your stand. There will come a time when you will be persecuted for even witnessing to My Name. Have no fear, as I will walk beside you on your road to Calvary."

Later, at the Cathedral Church of the Immaculate Conception, Portland, Oregon, I could see a large round church building. Jesus said: ***"My people, your churches have been beset by modernism. The advocates for change have forced renovations that have placed My Tabernacles in separate rooms away from the main body of the church. Many traditional statues and pictures have been removed as well as the crucifixes. This movement in My Church has tried to remove the sacred out of My Church and belittle My Real Presence in the Host of My Blessed Sacrament. I have died for you and I have left My Presence with you in My gift of the Eucharist. Do not be ashamed to give me honor and adoration. My Blessed Sacrament was not meant to be put off in a corner and forgotten. My children, you are about to be tested with a schism in My Church as Pope John Paul II leaves Rome. There will be two factions in My Church. One side will be led by the Antipope, who will control all of the church buildings and will mislead the people into following the Antichrist. The other side will be My faithful remnant that are loyal to the teachings of Pope John Paul II and My traditional Church. Both the laity and the clergy must decide whom they wish to follow-either Satan's Antipope, or My Gospel. You are choosing between the light of Me or the darkness of Satan. Those who choose Me will be persecuted, but they will be rewarded in My Heaven on earth and above. Those following the Antipope will be led straight to Hell if they do not change their ways. Worship Me only and never give allegiance to the Antichrist or take his mark in your hand or forehead."***

Monday, January 11, 1999:

At Holy Rosary, Portland, Oregon, after Communion, I saw a throne representing Jesus' power over everything. Jesus said: ***"My people, you are witnessing My reign over the earth and all of the universe. My power reigns over all of the angels and saints. There is no question about My authority over the evil ones. It is just a***

matter of time, until I cast them all into Hell and chain them there. Those who are faithful to Me have nothing to fear and a Heaven on earth will be their reward. So do not place any worry of earthly things in your path to Heaven. Everything on this earth will quickly pass away. Focus your life on loving Me and your neighbor and that will be enough for your salvation. My reign over everything is complete, and I am only allowing this evil to test your faith. Do not lose heart at what seems impossible to you. I will be protecting your soul against all of the demons. My arms of protection will shield you, as you will not be tested beyond your endurance by My grace."

Tuesday, January 12, 1999:

After Communion, I could see a tall arch on the side of a church and it was dark. Down the side aisle, which looked like a cave, there was a bright light shining. Jesus said: ***"My people, I am showing you the darkness of confusion that will come over a part of My Church. It will be My faithful remnant that will preserve the traditions of My Revelation. Modernism and a waning reverence for My Real Presence have captured the hearts of many attending church. Many changes in My Church have been inspired by Masons and there is a plan to play down the importance of My Real Presence in the Host. The promotion of Confession and the forgiveness of sins is lacking and many sacrilegious Communions are occurring as a result. I am showing you the light at the end of this tunnel to prepare you for My coming triumph. I am allowing this persecution of My remnant as a test of their faith. You are to keep focused on following My Will and preserving the true faith, and you will be saved. If I am with you, it does not matter who is against you. I love you all very much, and it is important to not despair in your trials. Have trust and hope in Me, and call on My help to guide you through this dark hour."***

Later, at Adoration, I could see a cross of light over a large gold serving platter. Jesus said: ***"My people, I was born a carpenter's son of little means, yet I survived in this world with little comforts. You people of America have become too attached to your possessions and comforts. I struggled each day for a living, but I never worried so much about tomorrow as you do.***

Many of you are not satisfied with just enough to get by. You have to have all of the new modern conveniences. You have been so spoiled with work saving devices; you are almost helpless at the loss of your electricity. It is for this reason of your greed for wealth and everything you could want, that your chastisements of the weather have affected your power outages. Instead of trusting in Me to survive from day to day, you have desired to have enough wealth to be self-sufficient. This is not trust in Me. You now place all of your trust in your own devices. As much as you think you are well off, I can touch you in many ways to bring you to your knees. Do not be so selfish that you hoard your riches to depend only on yourself. Those who have an excess should be concerned more with helping others. In this way you could be building up treasures in Heaven. If you are called from this life, to whom is all of your wealth going to go? It will not help you at the judgment. So, place your priorities on spiritual treasures instead of on earthly treasures."

Wednesday, January 13, 1999:

After Communion, I could see a little child being held. Jesus said: *"My people, in the Gospel I called the children to Me, because they have a special place in My heart. So, make a point to bring the children to Me at Mass every Sunday, even if they may cause some disruption. It is more important that they be exposed to My graces. In bringing up your children you need to give them a good example, by showing them that you practice your faith. By seeing that your faith is important in your life, it will give more reason for your children to believe as well. You have a physical responsibility to feed and educate your children on a secular level. Even more so, parents have a spiritual responsibility to feed their souls with the sacraments and educate them in the Faith. Each soul is precious to Me and you can dispose these souls to My love, but they need to be invited by you to My Kingdom. Once they reach the age of reason, they will be more responsible for themselves in coming to believe in Me. Even in the later years of your children and grandchildren, continue to encourage them to love Me and attend Sunday Mass. No matter how indifferent they may be, keep reminding them of their spiritual duty and be per-*

sistent in your prayers for them. These are your own children and you want their souls to be saved. So, be ever vigilant and lead them to My protection."

Thursday, January 14, 1999:

After Communion, I could see a prison door with bars on the window. Jesus said: ***"My people, a time is coming soon when people will persecute you for believing in My Name. Your evil age will grow worse with the coming Antipope and the Antichrist. Do not have fear, My faithful, for I will be watching over you with the help of My angels. These evil people will try to force you to worship the image of the Beast. They will also try to force you to take the Mark of the Beast. Some will be martyred, tortured, or enslaved. That is why I am showing you this prison setting. Those that go into hiding as Pope John Paul II leaves Rome, will avoid imprisonment with My help. I have gone before you and they imprisoned Me and killed Me on the cross. Since I had to suffer for your sins, you will have to suffer as well. Do not think if you take the Mark of the Beast, that you will avoid suffering. Those unfaithful to Me will suffer a worse pain when they will go through a living hell on earth with the plagues and an eternal pain burning in Hell. So come, My lovely ones, and share in My love and peace which you will be rewarded for in My Era of Peace on earth and My beatific vision in Heaven."***

Later, at the prayer group, I could see a table with champaign glasses for a wedding. Jesus said: ***"My people I have invited My chosen people to come to the wedding feast, but few are accepting my invitations. So, I sent out My prophets and messengers to invite even the Gentiles to My wedding feast. I have not told you the date of My triumph, so you must be vigilant in your preparations. By frequent Confession, you can have your souls ready for Heaven. But if you fall into sin without being prepared in a proper wedding garment, you will not be allowed entry into My banquet."***

I could see some gold rings and some tall business buildings. Jesus said: ***"My people, your monied people have lost a sense of reality in their greed in the market place. Even though there are ominous signs in the world economy, they still talk of expected*** *profits. These markets will be brought low as your country will be brought to its knees through the loss of your possessions. Seek to rely on Me only, rather than your elusive wealth."*

I could see an angel in the sky over many people at a refuge. Jesus said: *"My people, I have told you that you would be protected at My places of Holy Ground and places of My Mother's true apparitions. You are seeing the angel that will be visible at My safe havens. Their power will be great over the evil ones and the people will witness My glorious triumph. Rejoice that you are living in these wondrous days."*

I could see a child stare blankly seeking a mother's love that never came. Jesus said: *"My people, respect the job you have been given as parents. It is better to give your love to your young children, rather than seek jobs to have more riches. Money you can always have, but the years of bringing up your children are over quickly. Do not expect your children to learn of the faith from others. Your best way to build up faith in your children, is to teach them first hand by your example and teaching. When you come to your judgment, you will have to account for how you led these souls and cared for them."*

I could see Mary dressed in blue with a crown. Mary said: *"My dear children, pray for your Holy Father in Rome, for he is being tested by those around him. His time is short, as he leads his flock to follow the way of life I have shown you. Every moment you have him in your service is precious. His reign has brought a new awakening of faith to my Son's Church. He suffers in many ways to provide his leadership for your age. Continue your prayers so he can complete the task that he has been given."*

I could see Jesus up close on the cross as He was being taken down. Jesus said: *"My people, you have just shared in My love and peace of the Christmas season. Soon you will be coming again to another Lenten season. This time of reflection coincides with your new resolutions that you have been contemplating. You need to be moving forward in your perfection and follow My Will. Start to plan now how you can improve your spiritual life so you can have a plan to go forward when Lent arrives. These moments of reflection pass quickly, so the longer you dwell on this subject, the better prepared you will be in growing this Lent."*

I could see a bird flying over an orange sky. Jesus said: ***"My people, I have told you many times to look to the skies for the signs of your times. Many heavenly bodies have traversed your skies giving you signs, if you were attentive to them. I have shown you many comets and changes in the stars. The colors of the sky also will foreshadow the events of the tribulation. Look for your comet of chastisement, for it will soon be visible and recognized by all. You have explored the planets and stars for your own gain, but you fail to see how My Scriptures will be fulfilled in these signs of things to come."***

Friday, January 15, 1999:

After Communion, I could see doctors standing in a circle in an operating room about to perform an operation. Jesus said: ***"My people, I am portraying your country in this vision of an operation in a hospital. You think that you are in control of yourselves, but I will bring you to your knees with both the weather and your own man-made problems. These weather extremes of hot and cold are like your spiritual lives, neither hot nor cold. They are a result of your pollution and your own scientists manipulating the weather for their own agenda. There are forces in your world working to take over everything in preparation for the Antichrist. By creating financial crises and physical instability with your infrastructures, these evil men will use these excuses of terrorism and looting to call martial law. In this way all of your rights will be lost to a police state, which will usher in your tribulation. This winter season will be one of your worst in preparation for many events to come. Prepare spiritually and physically with My help and you will endure this trial. You will suffer for a while, but My triumph is coming soon and all of this evil will be cleansed from the earth. Satan's reign will be brief, as My victory will be his downfall. You, My faithful, will then rest in My love in peace on earth and in Heaven."***

Saturday, January 16, 1999:

At the Carmelite Convent, St. Catherine's, Ontario, Canada, I could see a chair with Jesus' face on the back and then there were some Carmelite nuns present. St. Therese came and said: ***"My dear*** *children, the contemplative life is a blessing not only to live, but its purpose is to pray for sinners to be saved. The saving of souls, as you know, has always been my one duty to Jesus that I treasured in my heart. We have taken a vow of poverty so that we are freed of the entanglement of possessions, where everything is held in common. We also have taken a vow of chastity, where Jesus is our only spouse. We did our prayers and our daily chores with delight, since we did everything for the sake of Jesus. It is good, my children, to spend time with your Savior, Jesus, in quiet meditation. Jesus loves you all so much and you need to take time to show Him your love in your prayers and your deeds. Jesus sees all that you do and He will reward you for serving Him. Never lose heart in your troubles, but turn to Jesus for your help. Do not let little things disturb your peace, but see them as tests of your faith in our Lord. Spend all of your time in the service of Jesus, not wasting a precious moment. Remember constantly your purpose for your being here and let Jesus walk with you on your road to Heaven."*

Sunday, January 17, 1999:

At St. Francis Xavier Church at Mississauga, Ontario, Canada, after Communion, I could see a white cross without a corpus. Later, I could see the suffering Jesus on the cross. Jesus said: *"My people, I am showing you the cross without the corpus, because some people think they do not need Me in their lives. Some are coming to Mass, but they go through the motions and they go about their lives the rest of the week without thinking of Me. Even if you do not give Me the glory due to Me, I am the one who provides everything for you, even your very life. So, put me back in your lives by placing My corpus back on the cross. Open your hearts and let Me in to be with you every day. By your daily prayers, you invite Me into your lives so I can be a part of every day of your lives. I do not force My love on you, but I invite you to love Me. When you seek My Kingdom first in your lives, everything will be given you. So, rejoice in the joy of My love and peace that I rain down on all of My faithful. With Me at your side, you have no worries about your soul being protected from the evil ones."*

Monday, January 18, 1999:

At St. Mary, Queen of Creation, New Baltimore, Michigan, after Communion I could see a triangle representing the Trinity. Jesus said: ***"My people, there is mention in the readings about the order of Jewish priests from the time of Melchizedek. Since I have existed from all time and I came to man to offer My life for your sins, I have been the first priest since I instituted My Sacrament of Holy Orders. At the Last Supper I gave you My first service of the Mass in offering My Body and Blood up for your sins. I then fulfilled that sacrifice with My death on the cross. The priests in My Church now offer up My same Body and Blood for you in an unbloody manner for the forgiveness of your sins. I give you My Real Presence in the consecrated bread and wine. Your priests are still offering the Sacrifice of the Mass and do not think that you are just offering up only a meal. This is more than a meal, for in My Eucharist, it is My own Body and Blood that I offer up for you under the appearances of bread and wine. This Transubstantiation of these species into My Body and Blood is a miracle of My grace that I have left My Presence with you to the end of this age. Give thanks to Me for My loving sacrifice of My life that you may be saved and redeemed of your sins. You are given the opportunity to come to Heaven and be with Me forever. Accept Me as your Redeemer and seek the forgiveness of your sins in Confession. Then I will welcome all of My faithful into My Heavenly Banquet to enjoy forever your presence in My One Being."***

Tuesday, January 19, 1999:

After Communion, I could see a cross of two white lines without the corpus. Jesus said: ***"My people, why do you want to strip My Body from the cross? A cross without Me dying on it, means nothing. You cannot have a resurrection without My Crucifixion. The reason for displaying My cross is to show you how much I love you by dying for your sins. If you cannot see My Body, you will soon forget what I have done for you. So, do not let people convince you to take My Body off the cross and struggle to keep this picture before you. There are some evil forces at work to take away all reverence of My Host and Blessed Sacramentals. They*** *are the same ones removing My Crucifixes and the statues of the saints and angels. These evil ones do not want My manger scenes in public, nor any religious mention of My Commandments. The condemnation of your nation comes in your placid acceptance of the removal of all that is sacred. You must stand up and be counted among My faithful or you will fall into the hateful hands of Satan, who wants to destroy you. You must struggle to do good and follow My Will in saving souls or many of you will be lost forever in Hell."*

Later, at Adoration, I could see the earth from high up and there was a volcano that let loose with an explosion of rock and lava. Jesus said: *"My people, I am showing the eruption of this volcano, because you are going to see an increasing frequency of these events. As more earthquakes occur, they will trigger more volcanic action. Each one of these eruptions has had a devastating effect on the landscape around them. The dust that they carry high into the sky will cause different colorations in the atmosphere and a dimming of the sun's light. Prepare for these events by perfecting your life in constant Confession so you will be ready for My coming again in triumph. No longer do you have the luxury of coming to Me in conversion at your own time. Your time for conversion is running out, so work on saving souls as soon as possible. Those seeing these events will be greatly shaken, so they will be open to your evangelization efforts. Take advantage of every opportunity to bring souls to their salvation in Me."*

Wednesday, January 20, 1999: (Dean's funeral Mass)

At St. Mary's Church Rexville, New York, after Communion, I could see a long corridor with many different shelves of life's experiences. Jesus said: *"My dear friends, thank you for sharing in Dean's leaving, but also to be joyful in his rising to Heaven. He is with Me now and he is comforting his family with his prayers for you. Dean has suffered much in his trials and the prayers said for him were a help to sustain him in his pain. His life is truly a gift to all of you as every life is a gift to each other. This vision, I am showing you, is to relate to your life as you go through life taking your place in My plan. Each step of your life is a new beginning where you share life's trials and joys with those you*

love. It is sometimes a loss for some who do not fully experience all of life's experiences, but you can be thankful for even a shortened life. Through every experience in life I am there for each of you. I have laid out a plan for each life and it is your acceptance that I seek to follow My Will. Death is a part of your life, even though it be difficult at this separation. You need to die in the body, so your spirit can be raised up to Heaven. You cannot experience your resurrection unless you suffer your Calvary in dying. After each soul is tested, I hold My arms out to greet you as you approach your judgment. Dean can now draw close to My bosom where He shares in My peace and love forever. Your spirit lives on in My love, so do not be saddened at one's death. I am comforting all of you with the joy of Dean's coming to Heaven and I offer you the same invitation of following Me to Heaven."

Later, at Adoration, I could see many dark claws reaching to destroy the light. Jesus said: ***"My people, this vision represents how evil is closing in on the light of faith so they can attempt to remove the faith from My people. You are protected by the light of faith if you do My work. As the evil darkness gains control of your world, there will be a darkness of sin all over. The Antichrist will have a brief reign as evil will reach a level that you have never witnessed. But do not be concerned, because his power is under My control. I will then bring My triumph upon this evil lot as they will suffer a Hell on earth before they are chained in Hell. Follow My ways and I will read your heart and know of all of your intentions to do good. Fear not this trial which is about to come, because you will grow stronger in My love as you are tested. You will be led by your angels to safe havens and I will provide for all of your needs. My love will conquer all and then you will share in My peace in the light."***

Thursday, January 21, 1999: (St. Agnes, martyr)

After Communion, I could see some bunches of new flowers blooming. Jesus said: ***"My people, you are appalled to think of the martyrdom of a young girl as in today's St. Agnes. The vision shows you how this life was snuffed out before it could even come into full bloom of the plan I had for this girl. You should be equally appalled at all of the little lives being martyred by your sins of*** *abortion. Not only is this holocaust evident in your own country, but it is even worse in the rest of the world. In some countries abortion is at such a rate as to even threaten the decrease in population. You have become so obsessed at controlling your family sizes, that you do not care about these atrocities against Me. You have been upset with the brutal killings of Kosovo, yet why do you have no feelings for the millions of My babies you kill every*

day? Because you do not always see these little bodies destroyed, you have put it out of your mind. Think of the filled garbage cans and other ways these babies are used for cosmetics and you know why My justice is coming soon to condemn you. Do everything in your power to protest this carnage and discourage these mothers from committing these mortal sins of killing against Me."

Later, at the prayer group, I could see a guardian angel pick up some little children. Jesus said: ***"My people, I send you My angels to guard you from the day of your conception. These angels will protect the little ones, especially during the tribulation. There will be some people and children martyred for the faith, but they will instantly be saved by My grace. Do everything you can to teach your children the faith and protect them from bad influences of sin. I love the children very much and woe to the person who would harm one of My children."***

I could see a picture of some towers and people in high places. Jesus said: ***"My people, those in high places are just as vulnerable to sin as anyone else. There are not two standards as one for the rich and another for the poor. Everyone is liable to judgment and must answer for their sins. Your justice system is corrupt in its practices as the rich and famous appear to get special treatment. It will not be so on the Day of Judgment. My justice and mercy falls on everyone equally. Those crimes on the earth will be answered for in Purgatory or Hell, even for those who seemingly have not paid for them on earth."***

I could see a red light on a road with the justice of scales being held in the balance. Jesus said: ***"My people, I have asked you to stop your abortions for many years. Yet you continue on your killing ways not taking heed of My warnings. The angels of the babies killed in abortion are many as they attest to your crimes. Your representatives have given a deaf ear to My pleas, so they can be politically correct, but they are spiritually wrong. As more chastisements visit your land, remember when I told you that you would pay dearly for your sins. Your apathy to changing your sinful ways will be further testimony against you. America's moral decay is on trial and you are found wanting in my sight. Pray much that your death culture will be converted, or you will see more spiritual deaths drive you into the abyss of Hell."***

I could see a well decorated casket with velvet and rich trimmings. Jesus said: ***"My people, no matter how much money you acquire, it is never worth the loss of your soul. Do not go through life seeking only your comforts, for these things will pass away. While you are alive, this is the time to work on your salvation. When they have placed you in a rich casket, it will be too late. So share your wealth and do not hoard what you cannot take with you. Store your spiritual treasures of helping your neighbor and you will gain more than any other investment."***

I could see a plain cold throne with a dim light. Jesus said: ***"My people, the false man of peace will be cold and calculating with no love. The Antichrist will have one desire of ridding the earth of all love of God. The evil ones hate man and they will do everything to destroy him. The evil ones will control the money, jobs and food, but trust in Me to provide for your needs. Take nothing from the evil ones, for they will give you anything for your soul. You would rather die in martyrdom than give in to the evil one's goods. It is your spiritual life that is more important than your physical life."***

I could see some people sleeping on beds in the caves. Jesus said: ***"My people, there is safety in the caves of My protection, but you must seek My help to be saved. I will show you miraculous ways of keeping the evil ones from knowing where you are. Their devices and dogs I will confound in their futile searching. At your places of holy ground and the caves, the evil ones will not be able to harm you. Trust in My shielding you from harm and your faith will be your salvation."***

I could see some elaborate means of trying to preserve the dead. Jesus said: ***"My people, throughout the centuries man has gone to great lengths using all of his scientific knowledge to preserve the dead. In recent years you have used cryogenic means to preserve the body, thinking you may live again one day. All that you do physically will never bring immortality to the body. You have focused too much on the mortal body which passes to dust tomorrow, instead of focusing on the immortal soul's destiny. When you struggle to save the spiritual life of the soul, that is when you will see your purpose for being here. I love you all and My desire is to share My love with your soul for eternity."***

Friday, January 22, 1999:

After Communion, I could see an empty alcove and a statue was partially materializing. Jesus said: *"My people, keep your statues of Me, the saints, and the angels visible for people to see. Even in your own homes, you could display your statues and icons. Make a special place as an altar for your holy relics and statues to be seen. In this way you are honoring all of us and it keeps the thought of our help fresh in your mind. Call on My help and the saints as intercessors, so you can ease your own struggles in life. When you have so many helpmates, do not forget to request our help. Why should you go through life on your own, when you can have the heavenly court at your disposal?"*

Later, at Adoration, I could see a ship at sea and there were some large explosions high in the sky. Jesus said: *"My people, your country is being challenged in many countries, especially in Kosovo and Iraq. As the leaders of these countries are looking at your president's impeachment, they are testing your resolve in fighting. You are becoming overextended in your peacekeeping operations and soon events will get out of hand. It is My continuing plea that you pray for peace in the world, despite all of these hot spots. It only takes one miscalculation that could trigger a major war. As countries become more desperate in their economic problems, war might be sought as a way out of their situation. Seek to compromise these warring factions, or war could destroy some nations."*

Saturday, January 23, 1999:

After Communion, I could see an aisle between several stacks of moving stones. Jesus said: *"My people, I have told you that if there is no one to praise and adore Me, I will command these stones to come alive and praise Me. All of creation gives witness to My glory, yet the man, I created, has become too accustomed to his comforts to praise Me. Many have become weak in not attending church and they have grown lazy in their spiritual lives. Your faith was strong in the beginning, but unless you kept up your prayer life, you have diminished in your fervor. You are not static in your spiritual life. You will either be increasing or decreasing. Just as I can revive these stones, I wish to light a fire*

of faith under those who are complacent to their Creator. Realize that you are here as a testing place to see how much you love Me. In order to be ready for Heaven, you must gain in perfection by drawing closer to living in My Divine Will. This means living to follow My ways instead of your earthly ways. So get up and get moving spiritually, so you will be ready for your entrance into Heaven."

Later, at Adoration, I could see a beautiful church with leaf gold mosaics on the walls. Then it became stripped to become dark grey walls. Jesus said: ***"My people, you have seen the time of My churches in their days of glory when man made beautiful churches for love of Me and not love of himself. Now in your time, the churches are built more to honor man and his building skills. In the coming days evil men will completely strip My churches and leave them as dark grey hulks, good only for museums and places to worship the image of the Beast. Evil will have its brief day when all open worship of Me will be banned and My believers will be threatened with death. My power will then reduce Satan and the Antichrist to rubble, as they will burn in Hell. Then My triumph will bring about My new Jerusalem, as evil will be no more. Then My love and peace will reign and your joy will be complete. Those faithful to Me will receive their just reward."***

Sunday, January 24, 1999:

After Communion, I could see some waves of water coming into the seashore. Jesus said: ***"My people, as you watch the waves come against the shore, there are some beautiful images that you can relate to your faith. Waves striking the rocks are relentless as they beat them into sand. In some ways My desire to have you love Me is ongoing as well, as I am constantly trying to melt your cold and stubborn hearts. Every time you see a new wave coming, it gives a sense of renewal in your faith. Never give up obeying My laws and if you should fall, there is Confession to cleanse your souls. Water for My disciples also represents a new beginning as in Baptism. As you bathe in water and soap to cleanse the dirt from your body, so also the grace of Baptism washes away the filth of your original sin. So, look to your Savior in Me and follow Me as I asked My Apostles to give their lives to My service."***

Later, at Adoration, I could see many flowers in place for a wake. Jesus said: ***"My people, there are many difficult emotions surrounding a death, but every time you visit a funeral, it is a constant lesson about the body's mortal nature. As you look on each person that has passed on, you can think that one day you will be in that casket. It is good to remind yourself that you are here as a test of faith in following My Will. Look beyond the grave, because there is no hope in the body's death. Your hope can only be found in the new life of the spirit of the soul. For those who have lived an acceptable life in My eyes I will lead you to My Heavenly Banquet with the reward of My peace and love forever. Now is the time to change your life into one of love for both God and neighbor. Without love in your life and a hope in the next life, your earthly life would be unbearable without purpose. But there is purpose to your life and that is because I am the Almighty Director. You were created to be with Me in Heaven for My greater glory. If Heaven is your goal, then do not place much priority in staying on the earth for worldly purposes. Focus your lives on Heaven and when you die, it will be a heavenly transition."***

Monday, January 25, 1999:

After Communion, I could see a large building with flooding waters beside it. Jesus said: ***"My people, as one region of your country recovers from their snow storms, others are recovering from ice storms and unusual tornadoes. Events in your weather are continuing their destructive ways, because you are not changing your spiritual lives. As you commemorate the beginning of your abortion court decision, it was interesting timing of the destructive tornadoes in Arkansas. Here is a message to your President as the destruction came right up to the mansion he was in before being president. His abortion edicts were his first acts as president and now he is being tested with his impeachment. Many storms that you have received have been to areas deserving of punishment for their sins. You will pay both spiritually and physically for your sins. Do not think that you can hide from Me and that your sins are not seen. As Adam hid from Me in the Garden, it did not stop Me from banning him out of the garden to a life of***

hard work. I am merciful, though, in that I returned to redeem you for his sin and your sins. I give you many blessings for being faithful, but I can take them away when your sins continue."

Later, at Adoration I could see candles shedding their light on the darkness. Jesus said: ***"My people, I am the Light of the World that dispels the darkness. At My Resurrection it was the burst of light that created the image on the Shroud. I am the dawn of a new age of grace as mankind has been redeemed. Before your electricity and lamps, the darkness limited man's activities. You*** *see the value of light when you lose your power. I will be the light that will give sight to those of My Era of Peace, so that you will be able to see both during the day and night. I am the eternal light of Heaven that each soul witnesses at your death and in near death experiences. There is a long but finite light from your sun, but I burn without being consumed as God the Father appeared in the Burning Bush. There is a special glow of love that emanates from all of My saints and angels. When you receive your glorified body, your robes will be washed bright in My light of love. You, My faithful, should be persistent in the faith and shed your light of love on all those souls you come in contact with. Give thanks and praise to Me and I will lead you to follow Me in the light."*

Tuesday, January 26, 1999:

After Communion, I could see a large lighted aisle down a church which grew darker toward the back. I then saw a bishop going down a side stairs into a crypt below. Jesus said: ***"My people, I have been warning you of the coming schism in My Church, but it will come as no surprise to you. You already have many divisions in My Church which are apparent in those who do not follow My pope son, John Paul II. When this current pope is exiled, your schism will formally begin. The next pope will be an Antipope, who will dismiss many of My Church's long standing traditions and laws. This evil pope will accommodate every religion, but will relax the laws against the sins of the flesh. By his evil decrees, you will know of his ill intent to try and destroy My Church. When he promotes the Antichrist, there will be no doubt in anyone's mind of the evil nature of this imposter pope. Fear not, My faithful, for I will raise up My Remnant Church to carry on My valid Real Presence. It will be My loyal priests and bishops that will carry on My underground church. I will still be among you, supporting your souls even amidst the tribulation. I will strengthen you in this time to endure the trial of the Antichrist."***

Later, at Adoration, I could see a gold idol of a grass-eating bullock. Jesus said: ***"My people, this is a symbol of your bull mar-***

ket where your country has been preoccupied with nothing but making fast money. Your markets have grown so hungry for profits that they are dictating policy to every stock holding company. The greed for money has so possessed these people that they think then can do no wrong and the market will continue going up. These monied people are far from reality and the day of a major crash will strip them of everything. Do not hold riches and earthly things on a pedestal to worship. I alone am your God and these visions of grandeur are only an illusion of the evil one to destroy you. Your goal is to be with Me in Heaven and not to be rich on the earth. All this appearing wealth will disappear and you will have empty hands at the judgment, because of your selfish desire for comforts and riches. The only existence of lasting value is to be with Me in My peace and love. So when you see the worldly worshiping their money as a god or worshiping the image of the Beast, do not be distracted, but live only to worship and adore your God. Even if you must suffer for My Name's sake and give up your comforts, I will reward you for being faithful. In the end salvation in Heaven should be your only desire, because I have given you My promise. The glory and love in the beauty of Heaven will far overshadow any brief moments of earthly comfort."

Wednesday, January 27, 1999:

After Communion, I could see a horn of announcement and a picture of the pope. Jesus said: ***"My people, how well the prophets of old have spoken of this stiff necked people of America. You speak well with your lips, but your hearts are far from Me. Many of you are polite and are happy to greet My vicar on earth, but few listen to his words on abortion and euthanasia. You are like the people of My day who heard the parables, but did not comprehend the meaning. Even when your people do understand what My pope son is saying, it is as if he said nothing to their hearts. You commit many sins of killing My babies and the elderly. You have not allowed legal protection for these parts of your society. Because you continue in your sins and give a deaf ear to My pleas, you will suffer ruination at the hands of My weather chastisements and other events. Put your hands together and pray for your sins of abortion to stop. Without sorrow in your hearts, My***

justice will visit every phase of your life. My words and My laws will not be mocked, no matter what else you do."

Later, at Adoration, I could see a world leader at a table ruling as a king but the flags were not of a national origin. Jesus said: ***"My people, recall the previous messages and visions of the ten flags you have seen before. More recently I have emphasized that these flags represented large areas different from the current nations. Those of the New World Order speak of these ten regions as you have seen. My Holy Scriptures refer to a beast with ten horns which indicates the ten nations under the rule of the Antichrist. This world takeover is coming soon and it will occur as a chaos of wars and financial collapse will grip the world. Much of this will occur according to the plan of the One World people as Satan will have his last chance to control all of mankind. Have no fear of this Antichrist and his agents, for his reign will be brief as I bring My triumph to overturn evil. All of these evil men and evil spirits will be at once chained in Hell in readiness for My Era of Peace on earth. This will be the time of the new heavens and new earth spoken of in My Scriptures. All of these events will take place as foretold in the Scriptures, just as I told My apostles everything about My coming was fulfilled. All Revelation has been given you. It is up to those with a wisdom of faith to know and understand these events as they are now taking place."***

Thursday, January 28, 1999:

After Communion, I could see a church and a set of doors on the front. The church was then covered with increasing amounts of snow. Jesus said: ***"My people, I am showing you these doors because many churches are focusing on the Jubilee Celebration of 2000. My pope son, John Paul II has visited your country and he continues to warn your country to honor and have respect for life. This concerns your taking of life in abortion, euthanasia, and even the death penalty for crimes. Even though My pope son is having health difficulties, his message needs to be heard and acknowledged by your people and your leaders. Killing is not to be chosen by consensus or polls. It is a violation of My Commandments and My plan for these lives. All those you kill, leaves their blood on your hands and holds you spiritually responsible,***

even if you think your laws make it right. This age has turned the morality of My laws upside down. When you think it is all right because others are doing it, it still does not give you the license to disobey My laws. My laws are on a higher plane than your earthly laws which are only justifying your evil actions. Your nation is still accountable for these killings and the weather chastisements will continue to worsen. That is why this image of a bad winter continues to hang over your country. It is just a matter of time before your people realize that these disastrous events are a punishment for your sins. The more sins you place on the scales of My justice, the more you will have to answer for them."

Later at the prayer group, I could see some handcuffs and a handgun. Jesus said: ***"My people, listen to My pope son as he pleads with you to stop using capital punishment for a sentence. His claim is that it does not allow forgiveness and reform of the criminal. He even gave forgiveness personally to his own would be assassin in prison. The true understanding of My mercy shows you that any taking of life is forbidden. My pope son is only emphasizing this principle of My mercy."***

I could see stores being looted in the recent earthquake. Jesus said: ***"My people, take a look at what happens when disaster strikes. Instead of working to help each other survive the trial, many resorted to stealing and looting of any food they could find. As days of no food drag on, there is a cry for help that everyone can respond to. Share what you can to help these people eat and have water. If you are faced here with such shortages, you will see how the evil ones can control the people by controlling the food. This is why saving your own food and trusting in My providing for your needs is your only solution. When you call on Me in the tribulation, I will answer your pleas."***

I could see some young children taking their lessons. Jesus said: ***"My people, it is indeed the responsibility to educate your children, but even more necessary to see what they are being taught. It is not just the secular courses that they need, but your children need to be taught in a loving Christian environment. It is more important that they learn their faith than be smart in worldly ways. Education needs to train the whole person — both body and soul."***

I could see children's desks and the building they were using. Jesus said: ***"My people, in order to teach your children, it will require some financial help to provide for the structures and supplies that your children need. As you give support to their secular education, you also need to consider adequate support for My Church as well. Many have tithed or have given of their substance to support My Church, but others only give a nominal amount or from their excess. You will have to account for the support of My Church at your judgment. Now is the time to bring My Gospel to all who will listen. You cannot give too much of your time and your money. I see in secret and I will reward you accordingly."***

I could see many lighting candles for their intentions. Jesus said: ***"My people, many times there are things that go on in life beyond your control. It is when your trials of finance of family reach beyond your means, that you need to trust in My help. Those that pray and offer their intentions up to Me will be cared for in My way. If you try to solve your own problems, you may become more troubled. Instead, seek My help and that of your friends and your peace will return. These trials of life are nothing more than tests of your faith. It is up to you to stay close to Me even when the going is hard. With My help you will never be disappointed."***

I could see a lot of bicycle wheels. Jesus said: ***"My people, as your standard of living decreases, there will be less money for cars and gas. It would be good to have some alternate means of transportation in hard times. Bicycles may become more useful, especially if your oil supplies become threatened by your wars. You would be surprised how little you need, if you were to live in hiding or under the trials of your coming tribulation. Be ready to live a new existence without the comfort of today's possessions. Fix your gaze on holding fast to your faith in Me and that is all that you need for your salvation. The things of this world are passing away. Be content with your lot and strive to be rich in your next life in Heaven."***

I could see the soldiers coming to quell the looting at the site of the earthquake. Jesus said: ***"My people, as you come to the time of the tribulation, a similar chaos will be in progress. This unsettled condition will result from a planned destruction of your***

financial system and an installation of a police state under martial law. Through such controls, the Antichrist will reach out to take over your world as a diabolical dictator. Just as he will gain control, My triumph will rain down and stop him in his tracks. I love you all and I will bring all of My faithful to an Era of Peace. Be patient and persistent in your faith and your souls will receive their just reward in My love."

Friday, January 29, 1999:

At the Church of the Immaculate Conception, Boystown, Nebraska, after Communion, I could see two large arches of a church and there were two large black creatures there. The one seemed as the sign of death and the other as a sign of evil. Jesus said: ***"My people, you are seeing in these signs of darkness a coming time when the Masons will take over My Church. This will be a severe test in faith, but have no fear, for My remnant will survive this trial. This is a difficult message, but I am giving you this warning beforehand. My pope son, John Paul II, whom you have seen recently, has called your country to task for its sins of abortion and euthanasia. The evil ones in the Vatican will find ways to exile My faithful pope so they can install their evil Antipope. I am telling you to beware of the leadership of this Masonic pope. He will try and mislead My faithful and eventually prepare people to follow the Antichrist. For My part, I will raise up My faithful remnant who will remain faithful to Pope John Paul II. This will be an underground church because of the schism that will be brought about at that time. My Church will be split into those who worship man, the Antipope and the Antichrist on one side vs. My true Church that follows My teachings to My Apostles. Do not follow this evil pope who will only lead you to a spiritual death as in the vision. Only worship Me and pray for strength to follow My true Gospel of love. The evil lot follows the riches of the earth and the worship of idols and power. My elect will continue to praise Me and follow Me into the light of your salvation."***

Later, at Christ the King Adoration, Omaha, Nebraska, I could see a large mural of modern things on the wall of a church. Jesus said: ***"My people, why do you go through all of your life to make things complicated and man-oriented? If you read your Scrip-***

tures, I am asking you to only come to Me in child-like faith. My love for you is simple to understand, because it is unconditional and never ending. You do not have to please Me to have Me love you. I will always love you because all that I create is good of itself. I have created you in My image and with a free will so you can love Me by your own decision to do so. So, do not complicate your lives with your own agendas and your own interpretation of My Scriptures. If you love Me and seek the forgiveness of your sins, your faith in Me will set you free of the hold of your sins. My mercy is endless, even as I taught My apostles to forgive seventy times seven times. No matter how filthy your sins are in your sight, I still see the potential of every soul to be cleansed and made radiant again. Since Adam's sin, I know more than you of your weakened condition to sin. You will not be tested without a way out of your troubles. My help is just a prayer away. Depend on Me to get you through each day and you will always be in My peace. I cannot stress enough to you how important frequent Confession is for your soul. My grace in the Sacrament of Reconciliation is your life blood to be spiritually alive. When you are in mortal sin, it is as if your soul is dead and lifeless because grace is absent. Going to Confession is not a painful experience. It should be thought more of as a spiritual transfusion of your life blood in grace. So come, My children, to your loving Jesus who wants you to always be close to My heart. Do not listen to the devil who says you do not sin and he discourages you from spending time on Confession and puts it off. Listen to your Savior, who loves you so much, and come share the joy of your Master."

Saturday, January 30, 1999:

At St. Elizabeth Ann Seton Church, Omaha, Nebraska, after Communion, I could see myself inside a tall tent. Jesus said: *"My people, when you receive Me in Holy Communion, this is a blessed event for your soul. You become as the Holy of Holies, a Tabernacle of My Real Presence. That is why you are seeing yourself in this tent as if you were inside of My being as you will be in Heaven. Because you are so graced with My perfection, you also must prepare your soul for My entry. By saying your act of contrition, you show Me your sorrow for your sins. If you have seri-*

ous sin, then you must confess these sins to the priest, before you ask Me under your roof. Give My Host and My Real Presence the reverence I deserve because I am truly your God, your Redeemer, and your Creator. I am perfection and I seek perfection in your spiritual life as well. Follow My Will and I will guide you in your struggle to be perfect. By giving of your will over to Me and letting Me lead you in life's trials, I will walk with you on your narrow road to Heaven. Be persistent in your faith and trust in Me with never a doubt in My help, even amidst the most difficult of times. You will see by being faithful to My plan for your life, that you will always experience My love and My peace."

Later, at Christ the King Adoration, Omaha, Nebraska, I could see a bunch of roses but in the roses were the faces of souls. Jesus said: ***"My dear son, thank you for inspiring these souls to be with Me tonight. My love is always calling you to adore Me and give Me thanks for all that I have done for My people. The love that is shared through My faithful is an inspiration for others to seek My personal love as well. As you sit in the pews gazing at My Host, My rays of grace shine on you as you are rewarded for giving up your time in your visit. My adoration is a wellspring of love showing you My abundant gifts that are waiting to be given to all who seek them. You know that the hour is late and many souls need your work to spread My message to those souls willing to listen to My Gospel. I love all of My souls and you may be the one to invite those souls to greet Me that are calling out to be saved. Do not give up on any soul, but continue your struggle to bring souls to Me, and especially to Confession. This desire to save souls is burning in your heart so you will not be satisfied until you have accomplished all that I have asked you to do. As you drink in My opportunity of My grace tonight, be thankful to all of the souls that work hard to bring Perpetual Adoration to the souls of this church and other places of adoration. It is not enough to admire your accomplishments through My grace, but continue to reach out for all of the graces I offer you."***

Sunday, January 31, 1999:

At St. Elizabeth Ann Seton, Omaha, Nebraska, after Communion, I could see Jesus reaching out to the people and the children.

Then suddenly there was a block wall placed in between Jesus and the people. Jesus said: ***"My people, I am here to ask you to open your stony cold hearts to My love. By My Beatitudes today, I am asking you to live a new way of life in the spirit. Disregard the ways of the world and be only focused on following My Will. When you try and live in My Divine Will, you will be living the Beatitudes in all you do. When you love Me enough to follow My Will, you are obeying My two great Commandments of loving God and your neighbor as yourself. When you love Me, you will direct your spiritual life to imitate My ways in your heart and to give your will completely to following My Will. When you love your neighbor, you will be willing to do the corporal works of mercy and you will live My love in the world. This is why following Me is foolishness in the eyes of the world. But reach out to every soul and share My love with them. Look out not only to their physical needs, but seek to satisfy their spiritual needs by bringing them to Me. Your example in action speaks much louder than any words you could say. Those who see your caring love will recognize Me in your actions and they will be inspired to love Me through you. Give praise and glory to your God for showing you the true way of following Me to Heaven."***

Monday, February 1, 1999:

After Communion, I could see a corner with flames all around it coming up from Hell. Jesus said: ***"My people, you have heard of the legion of demons I cast out of the possessed man in the Gospel. I am showing you in this vision how the many demons in Hell will be unleashed onto the earth to test mankind's faith during the tribulation. I told you that the evil of the tribulation will be so severe, that you would not have to ask when is the tribulation? It will be because demons were released that you will need My help and that of your guardian angel in order to save your soul. Even though evil will have its short reign, do not be fearful, since I will always be available for your protection. It will be a combination of evil men and these demons that will direct the Battle of Armageddon against My holy angels and My faithful warriors. My triumphant comet of chastisement will then fall on the earth confounding all the evil people with darkness. All the***

evil spirits and evil people, refusing My love, will be separated and chained in Hell. I will then bring about My new heavens and new earth as My Era of Peace will then reign over the earth. Have hope and trust in My victory when I will cast the demons out and into Hell from which they came."

Later, at Adoration I could see a stairway with gold gleaming rails and walls. There was a large Arab man coming down the stairs. Jesus said: ***"My people, all that is attractive to the eye is not always beneficial for your spiritual health. Golden riches have an attraction on the outside, but they do not lift your spirit. I am the only one that can give your soul peace and satisfy you completely. Unless you seek to be saved by the power of the Son of God, you have no life inside you. There are many who have accepted Me as their Savior. Still there are large numbers in other religions who fail to honor Me as God over their lives. I have come to reveal myself in time as a man, and I have sent you My prophets and apostles to spread My Gospel to all the nations of the world. It is up to man's own free will to choose to love Me and accept Me into your hearts. Without this acceptance of Me into your lives, you cannot be saved. This is why I have asked all of My faithful to continue to evangelize My Word so no one can say that they have not heard of My Gospel. There is coming a time in your tribulation where those who do not believe in Me will persecute you and even try to kill you. This will be a test of your faith to risk death for belief in My Name. Just as I love all men, you must love everyone as well, even your persecutors. Love is the binding force I give you to share with your neighbor. So, pray for peace in your world, even when disbelievers in Me want to make war with you. You may not be popular to follow My Commandments, but you will please Me in remaining faithful. When I come again to judge the earth, only those who know and love Me will be welcomed into My Banquet."***

Tuesday, February 2, 1999: (Presentation of Jesus in the Temple)

After Communion, I could see two rocks and out from there I could see a circling motion as a large propeller. There was a sound of buzzing with it. Jesus said: ***"My people, you are seeing again the sign that I have been giving you of the coming Warning. This***

circling of events represents someone's lifetime as it is flashed before them at death and near death experiences. Everyone living at the time of the Warning will see this life review pass before them. This is indeed a mercy and help that I am granting each person before the time of the tribulation. No one can say they were not made aware of My existence and how their sins are viewed by Me. Everyone at that time will have a proper conscience formed knowing what is sinful and what is not. From that point everyone will be held responsible for their own acceptance of My love and their choice to seek the forgiveness of their sins. This will be My faithful's most opportune time to encourage those away from Me to repent and return to My sheepfold. This time of My Warning is getting very close and you need to have your souls prepared by frequent Confession. Those found with mortal sin on their souls at the time of the Warning will suffer a far more traumatic experience than those without mortal sin. Those in serious sin will see themselves as spiritually dead and face condemnation to Hell if they do not change their lives. Everyone, after the Warning, will return to life as you know it and you will have a short time for repenting before the time of the Antichrist begins. This truly may be each soul's last chance to come to Me before it is too late and they are lost to the Antichrist. Pray much for the grace of souls close to you to be saved by this grace of the warning and the grace of My mercy."

Later, at a private home Mass I could see a circular window with shades and sunlight coming through. Jesus said: ***"My people, this window represents the light of My Word. Some leave the window wide open, since they would like to receive all of the graces that I am pouring out. Others find My light too bright and they want a part in leading their lives. These have the shades half drawn. Still others refuse to hear My Word and they are not open at all to let Me come into their hearts. These have the shades drawn completely down. The idea of home Masses may become more a part of your lives as the schism will become more prevalent in My Church. Those in the large churches will choose to follow the Antichrist, which would force My remnant into more home Masses. I will not leave you orphans, but I will have My angels deliver you Spiritual Communion of My heavenly manna***

on your tongues, where there is no Mass. During all of your tribulations, you will need My grace to remain faithful to My Gospel, no matter what the Antichrist may offer you."

Wednesday, February 3, 1999: (St. Blase)

After Communion, I could see people standing in the pews. Jesus said: ***"My people, I am deeply saddened by the attitude of My priests and laity for their lost reverence for My Blessed Sacrament. Part of this has come about because these same people have let their prayer lives dissipate to almost nothing. My prayer warriors and those adoring My Blessed Sacrament are the ones protecting the faith and holding up the scales of My justice. It is sad in this age of apostasy that even some of My priest sons would discourage the Rosary or adoration of My Blessed Sacrament. Your age has lost its sense of sin and your people no longer see the need for prayer and Confession of their sins. It is bad enough that some do not fully believe in My Real Presence, but it becomes diabolical when they deny My faithful the right to pray in church and adore My Blessed Sacrament. Faith in both My priests and laity is waning because the evil one has darkened their souls in their love for Me. If you truly love Me, you would show it in your actions and your prayers. If you are just going through the motions, then your heart is far from Me. This is the beginning stages of your persecution in the coming schism when you can no longer practice your traditional faith. Soon, you will only be able to pray in secret as people will become ruthless in torturing and killing My faithful. Do not complain, but ask for My help to sustain you through this evil age. You will only have to endure this for a brief time. Then I will bring My triumph to the earth and all of those lukewarm and those rejecting My love, I will vomit from My mouth into the flames of Hell. My priests will be held more accountable for their actions, especially if they mislead innocent souls. Continue your devotions in your prayer lives, since that will be your strength through all of these trials."***

Later, at Adoration, I could see clouds hanging low with embers of a church falling after being burned down. Jesus said: ***"My people, persecution of My faithful is beginning on all sides both from outside and inside of My Church. Enjoy the freedom you***

have to adore Me and receive Me in Holy Communion, because these will be taken away from you. The schism is already present in My Church. It will be My pope son's leaving that will bring about the formal split in My Church. The new Antipope, once placed in office, will begin making concessions to the worldly government of the New World Order. He will so want to protect his power base, that this evil pope will accept the Antichrist's demands of placing the image of the Beast on all of the altars. Those churches that refuse this demand will be burned to the ground. The evil of the tribulation will grow so great that the Antipope will encourage the people to even worship the Beast. There will come a separation of the faithful remnant from the evil lot listening to this Antipope. Do not follow this evil pope who will be misleading the people. Instead, follow My Will and be faithful to the proper teaching of the faith in My Church and the Scriptures. Be persistent in your prayers and place your full trust in Me."

Thursday, February 4, 1999:

After Communion, I could see a globe of the earth and it was in partial darkness. Then I could see an airplane with its engines on fire. Jesus said: ***"My people, you will be in a dim light, since many problems will develop in your computer controlled devices. The only dated devices working will be the ones that are re-programmed or where the internal dates have been set back. These problems will be world wide, as that is why you are seeing this picture of the globe of the earth. In addition to internal faults with your computer chips, there will be many manipulated problems in order to enhance the chaos of this year change. These problems will be much more pervasive than anyone could have conceived. These problems will take a lot longer time to fix than anticipated. Many of your travel, power, and communication systems will be affected. You will have to resort to your crude systems before your computers started. This situation and your ongoing wars will give the One World people an excellent opportunity for world takeover. These disruptions in service could well start occurring before the end of the year. Many government operations and your local infrastructures will be tested to the ex-***

treme. These problems may even cause martial law to be invoked to control the crowds without food and water. Many hazardous problems will be occurring where chemicals and nuclear materials are handled. Pray, My children, for you will be tested dearly in this year. Without My help, many could lose their faith."

Later, at the prayer group, I could see the moon reflecting the light of the sun and then various faces of people were over the moon. Jesus said: ***"My people, look on the moon as reflecting My love as the light of the sun is reflected off the moon. You are seeing other people's faces, because I want you to reflect My love as well. You are made in My image to know, love and serve Me. Let others see My image in your actions and your desire to follow My Will."***

I could see a woman wearing a scapular and a crucifix. Jesus said: ***"My people, I am showing you an example to always wear your Blessed Sacramentals of protection. The forces of the evil one are great and you will need Me to safeguard you from the demons who are gathering strength in this evil age. My mother's scapular and My crucifix, especially the Benedictine crucifix, are valuable means of protection. As you wear these in faith, you will receive many blessings of My peace and love."***

I could see a man at his workplace with many pieces of equipment around him. Jesus said: ***"My people, I know you need to give your employer a fair day's work for your wage. But during your day, you need to take some time to remember Me, especially My Chaplet of Divine Mercy at 3:00 p.m. The more you make an effort to remember Me in prayer, the more graces I will pour out on your work. When you offer up each day in consecration to Me, everything you do that day will become as a prayer."***

I could see some beautiful trees and mountains with a blue sky allowing the sunlight to warm the heart. Jesus said: ***"My people, be grateful for the beauty of My creation that you can take time to visit. Just as you feel better on sunny days, it is easier to follow your faith when things are going well. It is when you are tested by life's difficulties, that your faith is harder to follow. Without faith you would be more devastated. Call on Me to help you and have trust that I will solve your problems. This is why you should strengthen your spiritual stamina so you can withstand the coming tribulation."***

I could see a church and on the outside wall shoes were placed by those who entered. Jesus said: ***"My people, when Moses met God the Father at the Burning Bush, he told Moses to remove his sandals because he was on Holy Ground. You do not observe this rite, but you should give My Blessed Sacrament the same reverence as Holy Ground. I am really present in every Consecrated Host. So treat My Host as if I were present in bodily form before you. Give Me praise and thanks for My gift of being present before you."***

I could see all of the preparations being made for Benediction with the monstrance, the incense and the candles. Jesus said: ***"My people, you take My Host in Holy Communion at the Mass and you are blessed with My graces of the Eucharist. If you want to have that moment of My adoration extended, you can bask in the joy of My light as you give Me reverence in adoring My Host. This gift of My Real Presence can be savored during Perpetual Adoration and Benediction. Encourage your priests to share My Presence with you during Exposition. Even if you cannot have Adoration, make visits to Me in My Tabernacle for I love to have My souls enjoy My peace and love."***

I could see three chairs on an altar for the priests while the tabernacle was in another small room. Jesus said: ***"My people, remember that you come to give praise and glory to Me and not just man or the altar. Your sense of understanding of My Real Presence is lacking in faith. If you really loved Me and treasured My Presence in the Eucharist, you would have My Tabernacles at the center of every altar. Because you are having Mass, it does not mean that I am any less present in My Host. So give honor and glory to Me by showing My people that My Presence is only that which makes your churches holy. If you truly loved Me, you would place My Tabernacles in a much more prominent spot to be recognized as your King and Redeemer."***

Friday, February 5, 1999:

After Communion, I could see a cavity for a statue and it was empty. Jesus said: ***"My people, why are you eradicating all of your Catholic traditions in your churches? In many places there are no longer any statues, kneelers or crucifixes. In these same***

churches you have placed My Tabernacles in back rooms. These churches are void of any holiness and are just four walls to look at. My people need inspiration when they come to church. By seeing My Tabernacle in view, they can kneel in adoration without guessing where My Presence is. For those who genuflect on entering My Church, they have taken away the reason that My Church is holy. Those promoting these changes have little regard for My Real Presence and are carrying out their own wills instead of My Will. By belittling the sacred in your practices, how can you increase your love for Me?"

Later, at Adoration, I could see a spear in the dim light of darkness. Jesus said: ***"My people, there will be continual fighting over land during this evil age. Peace will be very elusive, as various leaders sense your lose of resolve. You have the western nations facing the communist nations and the Arab nations. You have basically Christian nations against the atheists and other religions. You have many fronts of many nations that you are obligated to defend. As your nation grows weaker in its morals and more susceptible for an economic crash, there is less stability in your balance of power. You are bankrupt in your fiscal policies by the size of your debt, and the valuations in your companies are highly inflated. You have all the makings for a major depression and a world war. Your morals are even more bankrupt than your finances. That is why My blessings have been withdrawn and your weather is raising havoc with your possessions. Pray, My people, for you are in a desperate hour when the evil one is about to reach his height in power. All of My faithful will be tested in their faith by the coming persecution. Trust in My help and My miraculous power to overpower Satan and his demons. When all will seem lost, My triumph will defeat Satan and you will all live to see My glory in the Era of Peace."***

Saturday, February 6, 1999: (Dean's Mass)

After Communion, I could see a beautiful red rose over a closed wood grain casket. Jesus said: ***"My people, everything happens according to My Will, so do not question when certain people are taken in death. I have repeated to you many times how every life is a gift. It sometimes takes a death to realize how precious each***

gift of life is. Think of each life as an equal opportunity for you to serve Me and follow My Will. I alone am the author of life and I am the one to call My souls home. It is man in his selfish and cruel ways who interferes with My calling in the taking of life. The rose, you see, has been used as a symbol for life against those who would do abortions. Death is a fact of life, but those who bring it on sooner are called before My justice. Every soul should be allowed the opportunity for sharing life as you know it. To snuff life out is not your right and those who kill need to seek My forgiveness. It is the evil one who encourages killing in any of its forms. Do everything to preserve life, despite the promoters of your death culture. Your voice in protecting life is needed more than ever in your world. Stand up and be counted for preserving life, so you can counter all of the evil one's influence."

Later, at Adoration, I could see a man stretching up his hands in worship of the image of the Beast. There were strobe lights all around him holding him in a trance. Jesus said: ***"My people, there will come a time when people will be more taken up with worshiping the Beast instead of worshiping Me. In your time of the tribulation, you will have been warned not to worship the Beast, but still some will fall victim to praising his miracles and peace gestures. Through My prophets and messengers, I have warned you of this age when the Antichrist will claim to be Me. I have told you if some say I am here or in the desert, do not believe them. Of the day I am coming on the clouds in glory, no one will know the time nor the hour. Know that when I do come in triumph, all evil will be cleansed from the earth. When you see the trees budding, you know that spring is near. I tell you when the sun is darkened and the moon no longer sheds its light, know that the Son of Man is about to call all men to judgment. I will separate the wheat from the tares and My faithful will enjoy My Era of Peace."***

Sunday, February 7, 1999:

After Communion, I could see a hill with a salt vein in it and then Lot's wife as a pillar of salt. Jesus said: ***"My people, I have told you many times that I am the Light of the World, and through My Mystical Body, you are a light to the world as well. You need*** *to be a shining example of faith for others to follow. You are the salt of the earth as well. Those who are faithful to Me I have sent out as evangelists to preach My Gospel to all the nations. You, who have been brought up in the faith, are the only ones I can send out. You, for your part, must remain committed to following My laws and My Will. Who can I trust, if I cannot trust in you to spread My Gospel? Because you have been called by My love, there is only one choice to salvation and that is through Me. Those who refuse to believe in Me or who do not live My Gospel will be the ones I will turn into pillars of salt for their unbelief. These evil ones will be the deadest of the dead with no return to My grace, because they have rejected Me as their Savior. For these will have no more to receive than eternal suffering in the flames of Hell."*

Monday, February 8, 1999:

After Communion, I could see a darkness in the shape of a doughnut with a light being drawn into the darkness. Jesus said: ***"My people, I am showing you this black hole appearance as a vacuum drawing people into sin. Evil is pictured as the darkness and it symbolizes nothing or a void, because there is no reason to desire evil. The evil one uses earthly things and pride to seduce you into desiring these things more than being with Me. But once you sin, you feel very empty. Once you have been satisfied, there is no lasting effect. All the evil one can entice you with are passing things with no lasting value. I am everlasting and My gifts of the spirit fulfill your longing for lasting peace and My love. So, look to Me and I can feed you My heavenly bread and the living water that will satisfy your soul with a lasting love of My grace. You are an immortal spirit and you are drawn to your Creator, who is always loving you. Look to satisfy the spirit's desire of My love and peace. Do not let your earthly pursuits of the body be drawn into the hate of Satan to destroy your soul. Keep focused on a good prayer life and your soul will always choose My love over the hate of Satan."***

Later, at Adoration I could see an empty chair representing St. Peter's chair. Jesus said: ***"My people, I have been giving many messages to you through many messengers and still you are not*** *changing your lives. I am the conductor that even the evil ones are awaiting the signal to proceed. I have given you extra time to repent. I have given you many signs in the skies and even many chastisements in your weather. But still you do not understand how much your indifference offends Me. Many, even of my people claiming to be Roman Catholic, do not accept the teaching of My Real Presence. Others do not even see the need for going to Confession. Look around you and you can see the apostasy. You can see all of the signs of the schism already present in My Church. It may take the Warning to wake up many souls and it will take a massive effort by My faithful to get these souls to come to Me. I am about to give the signal for these events to come to their completion. My pope son will then be exiled and the Antichrist will come to power. Wake up My children before it is too late. How can I motivate you further to arouse you from your evil ways? I am about to give the signal to My angels as well, for they will enter the battle for souls at this last moment. Trust in My help where My grace is available to those who ask for it. I will always give you a way out of your troubles if you seek My help. Without My help, Satan will sift you. Prepare yourselves to endure these last days. Once they are put in motion, the events will be like a whirlwind."*

Tuesday, February 9, 1999:

After Communion, I could see a closed door and it was dark in color. Jesus said: *"My people, many times you close the doors both physically and spiritually to Me and your friends. Then when you are in need, you are either too embarrassed or too independent to call on Me or your neighbor for help. Keep the lines of communication open both to Me and your friends. Through your prayers and even your prayer groups, you can open your closed doors. There is a risk with friendships in that you are made vulnerable to reach out and help others or to be rejected by others. You have no risk with Me, since I will never reject you, even in your sin. So, as Lent approaches, take on an open door policy both with Me and your neighbor. Do not be afraid to open your heart in love. When you are more outgoing and willing to help others, you will gain many graces for following My will to be more loving. When*

you have helped someone, it is rewarding to you to see how much you are capable of giving. This joy of your sharing gives you just a glimpse of how much you please Me when I share My love and graces with you. Stay focused on loving Me and your neighbor and you will never close your doors again."

Later, at Adoration, I could see a priest place the Sacramentary on the pulpit. The priest gave an appearance of Padre Pio. Jesus said: ***"My people, you are taking too many liberties in the latest translation of My Scripture. Today, you are appeasing the gender nature of the Scriptures for a better hearing for certain women. Even this reason is a little shallow, since the Scripture writers wrote in a different culture from today. But tomorrow you have set a precedent to appease other lifestyles which are compromising the nature even of the sin of your times. The Scriptures were not written to make every one comfortable with the words, they were written as revelation for My plan of your salvation. To that extent My Word cannot be compromised. Instead of encouraging many viewpoints in your translations of My Bible, I would rather you keep the words written by the evangelists. My laws are not changing with the ages. They are forever a light for you to follow My road to Heaven. So, pray and discern over these matters in your heart."***

Wednesday, February 10, 1999:

After Communion, I could see several people kneeling in contemplation at Adoration of the Blessed Sacrament in a chapel. Jesus said: ***"My people, treasure the moments you can spend with Me at Adoration. You have been reading of how I created everything and now you are face to face at adoration with the God who created you. As you enjoy the comfort of your quiet time with Me, think to thank Me for all that you have been given, especially your gift of faith in My Real Presence. Since the time that Adam sinned, I awaited the years to redeem all of mankind. This I did when I came to die for you on the cross. This gift of My life for you is the most precious gift you could receive. I have loved you so much that I died for every soul that will exist. That is why when you come to share in Adoration, it is your way of thanking Me for your gift of faith. There should be more souls adoring***

Me with you as I asked the cured leper where are the other nine. Ask your friends to come with you to seek opportunities to adore Me in My Blessed Sacrament. Even seek to have more churches establish times of adoration, so all of My faithful can have the opportunity to adore Me. Those struggling for these hours of adoration will receive many heavenly blessings. Those who trouble themselves to make time for Me will receive your heavenly reward."

At Adoration, I could see some large winged insects flying by. Jesus said: ***"My people, I am showing you a taste of the plagues that will afflict man during the tribulation. My faithful, I have told you, will be protected at Holy Ground places and caves. Those who are unfaithful will have to suffer a living hell on earth before they are chained in Hell. You are seeing the suffering that these evil souls will have to face. This is another reminder to those who seek to worship the Antichrist in order to take the Mark of the Beast for buying and selling. The far worse pain and suffering are reserved for the evil ones. My faithful will suffer persecution, but not to the extent that the evil ones will be facing. There will be no escape for suffering, since this will be your time of purification at the tribulation. Those that follow Satan will suffer immensely forever."***

Thursday, February 11, 1999: (Feast of Our Lady of Lourdes)

At the prayer group, I could see a church sanctuary and there was money on the floor. This was followed by an appearance of blood all over that spot where the money was. Jesus said: ***"My people, some of My churches are more concerned with money and comforts than saving My souls. That is why you are seeing this as blood money in forsaking the mission that these churches were given. To feed my lambs is the responsibility of every pastor so that these souls may be nourished in My love. These are the priests who will have to answer to Me for their actions."***

I could see a winding stairway with a white rug all the way up. Jesus said: ***"My people, this vision of the stairway is to represent your way to Heaven. The white rug symbolizes the wedding feast that I am calling you to. The color white also means that you have***

to be purified with the proper wedding garments to come to Heaven. In all of your actions and deeds you must strive to live My Divine Will in order to be perfect and ready to greet Me. Use My Sacraments, especially Reconciliation, to prepare your soul for Me."

I could see some early preparations for an Easter decorated altar. Jesus said: ***"My people, in order to accept Me at My Resurrection, you must prepare yourselves during Lent. During this season, you should make a deeper effort to draw close to My heart and offer up your sufferings for Me. When you fast and consider My preparations in the desert, you can see how good it is for your soul to purge your earthly aspirations and replace them with heavenly goals. I love you always, and now in Lent you can witness your love for Me."***

I could see a grotto with a little window and Mary next to the water. Mary said: ***"My dear little children, this is a special feast for your country because of my coming as the Immaculate Conception. You know of the healing waters at Lourdes and now this will be a symbol to you of the healing waters that will also be present at your places of protection. I am a refuge for sinners and I will be helping you as a mother helps her children. Have faith in the power of my Son, Jesus, who will be guarding you even through your coming trials. Rejoice in my triumph and that of my Son."***

I could see some old ads on an older black and white TV. Jesus said: ***"My people, do not become so dependent on all of your latest electrical gadgets. I have given you several messages concerning how your technology will be your downfall. When you have depended on yourselves instead of Me, now you will understand why I am stripping you of your possessions. You have been too distracted by your world and through this Lent, you can bring your focus back on Me. You are still vulnerable to your storms and power outages, so see these things do not last. Search for Me in your life, because what I give you is food for the soul that is everlasting."***

I could see a night scene with the moon shining and a homeless person sleeping. Jesus said: ***"My people, you are surrounded with many creature comforts, but you need to share your wealth with those less fortunate. You cannot have an easy life on this*** *earth, since you were meant to suffer as I did. So, do not concentrate your life on building up your wealth, but use your money and your talents to help the poor. Your money will soon be worthless in the tribulation. So, take this opportunity to help your neighbor and store up heavenly treasures."*

I could see an outline of the United States and there was a white background inside the outline. Then I could see it up close and this background turned to black. Jesus said: *"My people, your people were very good, generous, and religious in your early years. Now at this time your sins have overwhelmed you and your selfishness and greed are causing your nation to be black in My eyes. It is your sins of abortion and your sins of the flesh that most offend Me. I am calling your country to repent of your sins and pray sincerely for the conversion of sinners. My justice has to be answered, because you are not improving your lives. Come to Me, My children, and I will forgive you, but come and follow Me."*

Friday, February 12, 1999:

After Communion, I could see pentagrams and occult symbols of the Mark of the Beast. Jesus said: *"My people, these symbols of the New Age and the occult with their stones, crystals, and pentagrams are all means to call evil influences in their worship of these things. You are hearing of the enticement of the serpent to eat of the condemned fruit of the Garden. Now, in your world this same serpent, Satan, will be offering you the Mark of the Beast for buying and selling as the new forbidden fruit. Read your Scriptures, especially in the last book of the Bible concerning this same Mark of the Beast. You are seeing these same computer chips being promoted for buying and selling. When they encourage you to place a chip in your hand or forehead, you will see how advanced the evil of your age has reached. The Antichrist will soon try to take over your world and try to force you to believe in him and worship his image. Refuse all of his enticements and only rely on My miraculous providing of manna, water and shelter. Take nothing from these evil people, even though your living will be crude in the wilderness. Those who violate My First Commandment by worshiping the beast will be tormented*

in hellish pain forever. A few moments of pleasure or comfort are never worth the loss of your soul or eternal punishment in Hell. Hell and Purgatory do exist and they are means of My justice. Do not believe theologians or others who say there is no pain in this purification of Purgatory or no pain in Hell. These are all lies and deceptions of the evil one. The serpent always paints evil actions as good to get you seduced. Listen only to your Lord and seek My sacraments that will feed you with the life of grace in the soul. My bread and My living waters of Baptism are your only way to life in the spirit."

Later, at Adoration, I could see an old Greek statue with a bright light shone upon it. Jesus said: ***"My people, I am showing you this old statue to remind you how hard a life people lived long ago. They were much more concerned with basic needs such as food, shelter, and finding work. They had very few conveniences and had to work long hours to make any progress. You in today's world have much more leisure time than those living years ago. You have even grown too comfortable with all of your toys and entertainment. You need to utilize your time more wisely on My behalf than amusing yourselves. You should use your extra time for a better prayer life and more projects to help your neighbor. Your most important work should be centered around evangelizing souls to come to Me and even to make your own life more spiritual. You are coming upon another Lenten season. This would be an excellent time to analyze how you spend your time. When you work harder to please Me each day, you will be storing more treasures up in Heaven and you will feel more accomplished. Learn from Me by putting your own cares aside and spend your short time here loving Me and following My Will."***

Saturday, February 13, 1999:

After Communion, I could see a triangle and Our Lady rose up from the middle of the triangle. Mary said: ***"My dear children, this vision pictures me as coming forth from the Trinity as I was especially prepared without sin. As you hear the passages from Genesis, Eve is the first to commit the sin of taking the fruit from the forbidden tree. As Adam concurs in this sin against God, they are condemned to die and are cast out of the Garden of Eden. I***

am the New Eve as I was purified with no sin to receive my Son, Jesus, into my womb. God cannot abide in sin or imperfection. By My following God's Will in giving my 'yes' to the angel Gabriel, I became the sacred vessel by which Jesus came into the world. It was through my Son's offering of His life up for all of mankind, that He now promises you life in His victory over sin and death. With my triumph of crushing Satan's head and my Son's triumph, the faithful will be brought back to a new paradise on earth. Then there will be no more pain or sickness and you will enjoy again the life of Adam and Eve before the fall. Rejoice in the victory my

Son has brought about and continue to be faithful to His Word in your prayers and deeds."

Later, after Communion, I could see a large gem sparkling with light from its facets. Jesus said: ***"My people, the Kingdom of Heaven is like a precious gem, that a man went out to sell everything he had to buy that gem. That is the commitment that I am looking for in all of My faithful, that you would give up everything to follow Me. I have created you to be with Me in Heaven. At Adam's sin, Heaven was closed to mankind, but with My death as an offering for your sins, Heaven has again been opened to you. All I ask of My followers is to accept Me as your Savior and to seek the forgiveness of your sins. Lent is your time for a deeper look into your spiritual lives as to how you can continue to improve. By your faithful perseverance in prayer, you can keep moving closer to your perfection in faith. Do not be concerned with your failures. I forgive a contrite sinner, so you can continue your struggle on your way to Heaven. No matter how many times you fall down, continue to pick yourself up and return to My love. Think of your Lent as walking next to Me in the desert as I prepared for My walk to Calvary."***

Sunday, February 14, 1999:

After Communion, I could see a baby being held in a small hut. Jesus said: ***"My people, I am showing you this baby as a symbol of new life in the spirit. When a person converts from a life of sin and repents of their wrongdoing, this is a new change in their lives. When they are absolved of their sins in Confession, the graces given them make them a new creation from their dead spiritual life of sin. This life in the spirit is the lifeblood of the soul. By your mortal sins, you die in the spirit, and by My forgiveness in the Sacrament of Reconciliation, you again have new life in the spirit. I look for your faithfulness in your pledge that you made at Baptism and Confirmation. You may have faults and break our love relationship, but I leave the door always open to you as the father of the prodigal son. See this Lent coming as a time to renew your faith in Me, and to resolve to get closer to Me in prayer and fasting. I will continue to forgive you of your sins, but you must be always willing to return to Me for forgive-***

ness. You will be rewarded for your faithfulness by sharing in eternal life with Me."

Monday, February 15, 1999:

After Communion, I could see a speaker from a radio. Jesus said: ***"My people, I want you to remain open to listening to My Word. Do not have cold hearts either to Me or your neighbor. Instead of continually talking or only asking petitions of Me, this Lent you need to spend more time in silent meditation. When you leave time for Me to talk to your soul, I can relay to you My Will which you need to follow. Take time to do more spiritual reading and cut back on the time you waste watching TV or on other amusements. Reading the Bible or other spiritual lessons will do much more for the benefit of your soul than your plans. Lent is your desert experience which you should use to improve your spiritual life. When you make your resolutions to give something up for Me, make it something you enjoy doing, so you will find difficulty missing it. By your acts of self-denial, be resolute in your Lenten promises to maintain them throughout all of Lent. Use these acts of self-denial so your soul can grow in its perfection. If you are not doing anything to struggle during Lent, you are passing up a wonderful opportunity to get closer to Heaven. Sharpen your listening by being quiet and make the extra effort to listen for My Will."***

Later, at Adoration, I could see a bare altar with an incense holder sitting on the floor unused. Jesus said: ***"My people, the altar in this vision is bare, because some of My priests are not permitting My Adoration, or even giving easy access to visits to My Blessed Sacrament. I have become a prisoner not even in the Tabernacle, but even in the Church where they keep Me out of sight. All of these ways of lessening the importance of My Real Presence is happening because some priests are lazy in the ways of the world and they are not attending enough to their own prayer lives. Even though there are trends to belittle My Real Presence, I rely on My faithful to urge their priests to have more hours of Adoration. These hours would be a blessing for your parishes. Seek Me in My Blessed Sacrament, so you can learn how to be holy by following My Will."***

Tuesday, February 16, 1999:

After Communion, I could see a party hat for a celebration. Jesus said: ***"My people, you have many traditions and desires which seemed to be centered more around the body, than the soul. Your Lenten time is a suffering for the body, but a joy to the soul. It is the restraint you are putting on the body that causes it to rebel. The body seeks pleasures and desires to be instantly satisfied in all of its wants. The soul is the opposite, since it seeks to please Me first instead of the body. That is why the desires of the body are always in conflict with the soul in its desires. Lent is a time that you can take advantage or not to grow in your faith. I have created you as a whole person, body and soul. Your soul is immortal, lasting forever. While your body, due to Adam's sin, is condemned to die after a few short years. Since the destiny of the soul is more important than the body lying in the grave, you should do everything possible so your soul can be with the Creator who loves you. I love you so much, as I have shown you by My dying on the cross for your sins. I want you to love Me as well, but I do not force your free will. To be with Me in Heaven, you are to struggle against the entanglements of the body. The evil one is trying to deceive you through the sinful desires of the flesh. That is why you need to be on guard of these temptations to sin. By your acts of self-denial and fasting, you can control your bodily desires. As you purify your intentions in what you do, you draw closer to following My plan for you. So, actually, you should be rejoicing more to suffer for Me, than to satisfy the body. The most glorious moment will be when you are resurrected up into Heaven. Prepare for this crown that awaits all My people who are faithful to My love and My Commandments."***

Later, at Adoration, I could see an old nun in a black habit at a funeral with flowers all around. Jesus said: ***"My people, when the religious give up their outward identity, they begin to question their inward identity as well. For years it was the daily regimen of prayer and sacrifice that held religious orders together. Today, many have lost their original fervor for My service, when they let the influences of the world control their lives. Everyone is being tested in the faithfulness of their vocations, both the married and the religious. This worldliness is what has caused divorces, and***

priests and nuns to leave their commitments. It is not enough to say you believe in My Name, but you must show Me your love in your daily actions. As with any love relationship, I am in the middle of this activity. The graces of the Sacrament of Matrimony are there for each couple to sustain them through life's troubles. When their love for Me diminishes, it diminishes the love between the two spouses. Your marriage without My help and love will be doomed to failure. The graces of the Sacrament of Holy Orders for the priests and graces for the nun's vows are all intertwined with My love. When they have difficulty in loving Me, they soon find a loss in their devotion and many leave thinking they have lost their purpose for being religious. Pray for your priests, nuns and those married to stay joined in My love. Once My love is unraveled, the seams that bind these vocations, no longer holds them true to their calling. Do everything in your own vocations to strengthen your love for Me and continue being faithful to your promises and vows that you agreed to."

Wednesday, February 17, 1999: (Ash Wednesday)

After Communion, I could see people receiving their ashes. Jesus said: ***"My people, today when you receive your ashes, this should be a sign of your commitment to take on your promises for what you will suffer this Lent. Be sure to take on something difficult for you to do, and not things that you are already doing. Let it include some extra spiritual reading or some time in silent meditation each day. Once you have chosen a penance, be adamant in carrying it out throughout all of Lent. You must suffer the trial of time which will test your perseverance. Remember your fervor today and continue to maintain it for these forty days. I spent this time in the desert to give you an example, so you will be stronger in facing your temptations of the devil. Remember the goal of your Lenten resolutions and fasting are to purify your soul, so you will be ready one day for your own Resurrection into Heaven. Prove your love for Me by making a good Lent."***

(Joe Murray's funeral) I could see some beautiful awards being given out. Jesus said: ***"My people, why do you seek the praise of men? Those who seek fame and fortune on this earth have their reward only here. But when you die, you are quickly forgot-***

ten, since you are seen no more. Any praise from men is fleeting and quickly fades away. Those who seek to follow My Will and witness to My Name do not seek fame here, yet they will be famous in My eyes. Seek to follow Me and your reward in Heaven will be beyond your dreams. No matter how much ridicule and persecution you must suffer on My account, do not give up the fight. Truth will win out and I will vindicate those who defend Me and My Word. Never fear what the evil one can do, but have faith that I will strengthen you with the words of defense. I will stand by your side in all of your battles. I only ask that you persevere in your spiritual resolve and continue to fight the good fight. Then you will receive your crown of glory and no one will deny your fame in Heaven."

Thursday, February 18, 1999:

After Communion, I could see someone carrying a golf cart and others rushing about their lives. Jesus said: ***"My people, what is it that occupies your thoughts? Is it sports, computers, or work related subjects? Think of all bodily life as terminal, since you are only on this earth for a few years. There is no more life for the body when it dies, but the life of the soul lives on forever. That is why the life of the soul is more important than the life of the body. If the soul is more important, then your thoughts to protect your spiritual life should occupy a higher percentage of your everyday thoughts. No matter how much wealth you acquire or how long you try to preserve your life, you cannot prevent the body from dying. So use this Lent to put your spiritual life in perspective to your earthly life. A rich prayer life with plenty of spiritual reading will gain you a lot more than accumulating wealth or amusing yourself with entertainment. So, seek Me in My love and I will provide for all of your needs."***

Later, at the prayer group, I could see the exhaust end of a spent missile. Jesus said: ***"My people, this missile is a sign to you how quickly plans can go awry and more serious conflicts can happen. In your quest to protect your oil interests and to stop dictators from attacking their own people, you are becoming mired in many ethnic conflicts. Many small ethnic groups are seeking independence, but it is impossible to compromise every situation.***

That is why your planned attacks are becoming more serious and still they have not accomplished the peace you seek. War making begets more hostilities and is never a lasting solution. Pray for My peace in your world and refrain from starting something you cannot finish."

I could see large electrical coils with high voltage devices. Jesus said: ***"My people, man is manipulating electrical devices to control people throughout the world. Your new inventions will cause many sicknesses and will be abused to even control your minds. The evil one has had a hand in the evil uses of these devices. There will be many controlled through their Mark of the Beast as you do not realize the potential of these devices. Remember never to worship the Antichrist nor take his mark, his food, or his jobs. You would rather be martyred than to suffer what these condemned souls will face."***

I could see multiple laser beams being used to burn cities and destroy buildings. Jesus said: ***"My people, there will be sinister men trying to take over your world under the threat of using these beam weapons. Most all of your new inventions have been used to improve your war making power. Evil dictators will exploit these weapons of destruction to force people into submission to their will. Do not take the Mark of the Beast that can be detected by electronic devices. Pray for My help as the evil ones are about to establish their brief reign. Fear not, for I will vanquish all of them."***

I could see a body of water covered with a red tide of disease and bacteria. This was one of the plagues that the evil ones must endure. Jesus said: ***"My people, when I come in triumph, I will protect My faithful from destruction. Those unfaithful to My Word and My Commandments will be judged unworthy and they will suffer a living hell on earth from many plagues. Those who think the Antichrist will save them are badly mistaken. This Beast will only lead unsuspecting souls to an eternity of pain and suffering. Those who trust in Me will live to enjoy My peace on earth."***

I could see a great light over Jesus as Elijah and Moses were next to His glorified body. Jesus said: ***"My people, as I showed My apostles the two prophets of the past, this was a sign of My glory to come. My Transfiguration was a sign to give My apostles hope***

so they would not waver in their faith when I was to be taken from them. A time is coming again when I will send My two witnesses to wage battle against all of the evil ones. Just as I waged war against the bonds of Satan on men, these two witnesses will also wage a righteous war against evil. Have no fear, My children, for I will send My angels to protect you and provide for your needs. They will lead you into battle against all of the demons."

I could see an angel on earth with a bright light going out from that angel. Jesus said: ***"My people, trust in My power over the evil ones. They are never a threat to you, if you follow My ways. Call on My help and that of your guardian angels in the coming tribulation. I have conquered sin and death by My sacrifice on the cross. Sin and Satan could never have a hold on Me. I will always defeat Satan in his plans against man. Believe in My power over him and call on My angels to come to your aid in your troubles."***

I could see major unrest in riots and looting. Jesus said: ***"My people, your coming trial will test your faith, because you have never seen the extent of this evil. You will not get through this tribulation without My help. Just when you think all will be lost, I will strike at a crucial moment to snare the devil and the Antichrist from their intent to destroy man. I will cast these evil ones into the abyss of Hell, and they will be chained there so they cannot come upon the earth. Be patient, My friends, even in the heat of battle, for it will not be long and you will witness My victory. Follow My Will and you will have nothing to fear."***

Friday, February 19, 1999:

After Communion, I could see a white mist and then a lighted cave. Jesus said: ***"My people, I was buried in the bowels of the earth for three days, before I rose gloriously from the tomb. Thus, during the tribulation, some of My followers will be protected in caves. My glorious victory will bring you out to celebrate My new Era of Peace. As I suffered My scourging and crucifixion, My faithful must suffer mistreatment in the coming trial. All that you will undergo will be a purification of evil from the earth and a cleansing of your desires for earthly things. Your comforts in life will be stripped from you, so you can be open to My miraculous protection, even at the height of evil's power. I will vindicate***

all who believe in the truth of My Words, and I will lead My angels in victory over all of the evil spirits and evil people."

Later, at St. Mary's Cathedral of the Immaculate Conception, Kingston, Ontario, Canada, I could see a cornerstone of a large church. Jesus said: ***"My people, I am the cornerstone of My Church, since I instituted it with My apostles as My successors. I have come in fulfillment of the promised Redeemer. In every way Bible prophecy must be fulfilled, because it is the inspired Word of the Holy Spirit. I have given you My Real Presence in My Eucharist and I will be with you in this way to the end of this age. I will never abandon you, since I am always with you. I ask all of you not to abandon My love, but to always keep Me foremost in your daily thoughts and actions. When you come to My Church, you can always find Me prisoner in My Tabernacle. Give Me reverence by genuflecting in My Presence. It is My Sacramental Presence in the Host that makes the physical church holy. So, give My Tabernacle a place of honor in My Church and do not hide Me away in a back corner. You are talking about your God and your Lord in My Host. So, give Me the honor and glory that all of My angels never cease praising. I love you, My children, despite all of your imperfections. Seek to love Me in all of your actions."***

Saturday, February 20, 1999:

At St. Mary's Cathedral of the Immaculate Conception, Kingston, Ontario, Canada, after Communion, I could see a black covered Bible and it was opened before my eyes. Jesus said: ***"My people, I have given you My inspired Word in the Bible, but you must open it and read of My Word. I have come as a man so I could reveal to mankind all that has been kept secret. Now, you know of My love for you. I love you so much that I even died for your sins. You spend many hours and years studying the things of this world so you are prepared for a trade or skill to earn your living. It is even more important that you prepare your spiritual life, so you are purified and acceptable in My eyes to one day enter Heaven. To be prepared, you must study My Word in the Scriptures, because I have given you an example to live a good Christian life. By studying My revealed Word, this is your preparation for your earthly life so you can bring it into conformity***

with My Will. You have to be rigorous in your courses to gain your degrees. In the same way spiritually, you must persevere in understanding My Word and My Will for your life. I love you always, My children, and I share that love in My Word. But unless you pick up your Bibles and study them, it is hard to know My way. Pray for discernment and understanding so you will live your lives in imitation of Me."

Later, at St. Thomas a Beckett Church in Montreal, Quebec, Canada, I could see a multiple number of caves in the desert. Jesus said: ***"My people, as you start your Lenten devotions, I bring your attention to the temptations of Satan in both readings. Adam and Eve were seduced by pride to eat of the tree of the knowledge of good and evil. In the Gospel reading Satan tempted Me with the desire for food and the pride of controlling the world. Satan is always tempting you. Since Adam's sin, you have been weakened to sin, but with My coming, I have given you freedom once again in My Sacraments. If you fall in your sins, you are not banned forever from My kingdom. Instead, you can come to Me in Confession to have your sins forgiven. As you are tested in your Lenten devotions, the thoughts of My spending time of preparation in the desert comes to mind. You will be tested in the coming tribulation, so now is the time to strengthen your resolve to follow My Will. At that time, Satan will tempt you at his height of power with a new apple of the Mark of the Beast. The desert scene is in reference to how I helped My people in the desert of the Exodus experience. I will call you once again to put your full trust in Me to leave your comforts and possessions behind so I can provide for your needs at My refuges. Call on Me and your guardian angels to provide you My heavenly manna. My people in the desert trusted in My leading them. Now, My faithful of today must trust in Me with that same full trust to fulfill all of your needs of food and shelter. By a miraculous physical sign you will be led to My refuges. Have no fear and come follow Me in faith."***

Sunday, February 21, 1999:

At St. Luke's Church, Montreal, Quebec, Canada, after Communion, I could see a skylight with beautiful sunlight shining in. Jesus said: ***"My people, as you see My beautiful sunlight and all***

of creation around you, you can see why I called it good when I created it. You are all beautiful creations of mine and I love you equally in My sight. As you look at the effects of evil in your world, they are all brought forward by the evil from people's hearts. The devil tempts you to do evil, but it is an assent by your free will that brings about murder, anger and abortions into reality. I do not leave you orphans. You can call on My Name and My help to resist these temptations. Even when you fail and fall victim to the evil one's temptations, you can come to Me for forgiveness of your sins in Confession. So, do not despair that sin is in the world or when you fall in sin, for I am the great healer and I invite you to cleanse your souls. By prayer and good spiritual practices, you can strengthen yourself against sin and temptations. It is through My victory over sin by My death on the cross, that I share My power of love with you. Think of sin as cold and hateful, for it cannot exist in the presence of My love. So, if you work towards loving Me and your neighbor, you will not give in to the desires of the flesh with its selfish wants. Focus on My love and My healing graces of My Sacraments and you will enjoy My peace and have no fear of the evil one."

Later, at St. Dennis Church, Montreal, Quebec, Canada, I could see an old church. Jesus said: ***"My people, your faith in God is a precious gift which you should treasure as a gem. Your faith cannot have a price, because it is your means to your salvation. It is important to nourish and maintain your faith with prayer and fasting. When you love someone, you do not tell them only once a week. Come to Me in daily prayer to tell Me how much you love Me. I love you at all times even in your sin, because I see a value in every one of My creatures. But man is special to Me because you are made in My image with a free will. I do not force you to love Me, but I ask you to love Me by your own choice. Seek My love and avoid the hate of the evil one who tries to deceive you. By being faithful to Me in life, you will live in My peace and love in Heaven."***

Monday, February 22, 1999: (Chair of St. Peter)

After Communion, I could see a hole dug at the side of the church and Pope John Paul II was going down a new stairs. Then I saw a black knife get stabbed into the chair of St. Peter. Jesus said: ***"My people, I am showing you how My pope son will be leaving Rome to form an underground church. Another will take his place after forcing Pope John Paul II into exile. The black knife indicates that the Antipope will have evil roots and he will have diabolic designs to change My Church. He will cause a schism in My Church by his evil decrees. His evil roots will be linked to his Masonic loyalties. Many of My Church's traditions will be rooted out and they will be replaced by man's laws and not mine. When this Antipope promotes worshiping the Antichrist, there will be no doubt of his evil intent to mislead My people. Everyone in My Church will then have to take sides either to Follow My Pope John Paul II or this Antipope. This great schism in My Church will lead up to the start of the tribulation. When you see My Pope son leave Rome, I have encouraged you to call on Me and I will have your guardian angels lead you to a safe refuge in hiding. Do not take the Mark of the Beast and do not worship the image of the Beast. Your faith will be tested when I strip you of all of your possessions. Follow My angels into hiding and I will provide for all of your needs. I have repeated this message many times, but soon you will see these events unfolding and you will be forced to believe this prophecy. Always choose to follow Me and you will be saved."***

Later, Adoration I could see vast crowds coming to football stadiums to hear and watch the Antichrist. Jesus said: ***"My people, you will see the Antichrist as the great deceiver, as he will follow Satan as a master of lies. By the Antichrist's charisma, he will draw many to hear him as a man of peace in the football stadiums. Many already have made sports their god, so that is why he will place his followers in a familiar environment. The Antichrist will draw many to believe in him by his magical powers. He will then seduce some people to worship him. He will then pass decrees that everyone should worship his image. Those who refuse will be put to death. Many of your dictators have already demanded their subjects to give them allegiance. By forcing people to buy and sell with his Mark of the Beast, he will try and control the whole population. I have called on My faithful to go into hiding away from this false christ's influence. Do not worship*** *him even under pain of death. Do not take his Mark or anything else he will offer you to control you. By remaining faithful to Me, I will protect you and provide for your needs at My places of refuge. Have hope and trust in Me so you can save your souls in this coming trial."*

Tuesday, February 23, 1999:

After Communion, I could see a white arrow point straight up. Jesus said: ***"My people, I am showing you the one way street to Heaven. If you truly love Me, you will do everything on earth to gain Heaven. You need to keep this goal in focus no matter how many times the devil will try and distract you. I created you to be with Me forever and your soul will never find rest until you are with Me. Your soul seeks to be with Me, because it desires to rejoin its master. My love and My light are as a beacon drawing souls to Me. If you knew anything of Heaven's delight, you would have no other goal than to be with Me. Think of the purpose in everything you do. Unless it leads you to Me, then avoid all other distractions. With My signpost in your constant vision, you can test all that you do by whether that will bring you closer to Heaven. Seek Me in your prayers, your adoration, and the forgiveness of your sins in Confession."***

Later, I could see a large A and a large omega of Greek letters. Jesus said: ***"My people, I am the alpha and omega, the beginning and the end of all creation. I am from the beginning and I exist now and forever. I created man in the beginning of the earth, but I had to banish him from the Garden of Eden, because of his disobedience to My Will. I came in the flesh as a man to atone for all of mankind's sins and I died for all of you in or-***

der to open the Gates of Heaven. I will come again to remove all evil from the earth and I will bring an end to this age of apostasy and sin. There will then be a new beginning of an Era of Peace, as man will once again witness My Garden of Paradise. I will give you a life that is long and with full knowledge, so you can experience the earth as I originally created it. There will be no fighting and you will want to adore Me as the angels do. At the end of My Era of Peace, I will resurrect every body that existed, so they could be reunited with their souls at My last judgment. Then the eternity of My heavenly court will begin, where all of My faithful will witness My Beatific Vision. You will then share in My love and My peace where only I can satisfy your soul. Rejoice, My people, that you will live to see My day of glory."

Wednesday, February 24, 1999:

After Communion, I could see some relics in reliquaries. Jesus said: ***"My people, I am showing you these holy relics as something you should treasure and revere. These are more than just statues or icons. They are the very bones or clothing of the saints. You should give them proper reverence by making them available to be seen. Pray to the saints as intercessors for your petitions. The more you have faith in your prayers and your petitions are said according to My Will, the more they will be answered. Take time to properly display your relics for all to see. They are not meant to be stored in a drawer out of sight. Take care of them so they are not lost or abused. By your proper reverencing of these relics, many blessings will be afforded you."***

Later, at adoration, I could see darkness and houses were burning all around me. Jesus said: ***"My people, do not get comfortable with the things around you. There will come a day when your possessions will be stripped from you. You may even see all that you have worked for, go up in flames in a burst of rage against you. My faithful will be persecuted by ruthless dictators, who are seeking to control everyone. They will think nothing of killing those who stand in their way to world control of man. That is why I am preparing you to be detached from this world's goods, because they will be quickly passing away. When you are resolved to do only My Will, you will not be distracted by anything of this*** *world. Keep your focus on Me and you will see that having My love is all that you need. I will take care of My own and then I will seat you in a place of honor at My wedding banquet."*

Thursday, February 25, 1999:

After Communion, I could see a skull and then a fast movement through valleys and mountains. Jesus said: ***"My people, a soul roams through their whole life searching to find Me. You do not have to go far to find Me, because I am always at your side. Your search starts first as you try to satisfy yourself with the things of this world. This is a harder lesson for some, because My peace and love cannot be found in materialism. No matter how much you seek Me in things, you will only find emptiness and disappointment. That which I have created is beautiful to see and touch, but those things of man have been corrupted. So, seek My love and peace in My sacraments. My Real Presence in My Eucharist awaits your discovery that My food is the only food that can satisfy your soul. When you truly find Me in faith, you will never want to leave Me. As you search for Me, you seek in vain if you only want to seek worldly things. Seek Me, who is everlasting, and I will give eternal rest for your soul. Those who find Me in faith have the most precious of gifts that you can have — My own Divine Person."***

Later, at the prayer group, I could see a king dressed in gold. Jesus said: ***"My people, you have made money and possessions your god. You respect people by how rich they are and how much influence they have. My disciples cannot have such gods before them, because you are to worship Me only. I love you, My children, but I love you unconditionally, not by how successful you are. The world measures your worth by your money, but I measure your love for Me and your love for your neighbor. You work to provide a living, not to acquire riches beyond your needs. You should share your wealth with the needy and not use it for selfish pleasures."***

I could see some people in some pews of an older church. Jesus said: ***"My people, you have many wonderful traditions during your Lenten season. Use this time for your spiritual growth. After each week, review your progress in what you have set out to***

accomplish. You may have to make some changes in your attitudes if you are to really improve your spiritual lives. Take this time to review your worst sins and work on some practical means of avoiding these temptations. Remove yourself from any environment that may lead you to sin. Do everything you can to form a right conscience so you will know what offends Me."

I could see someone hiding in the darkness because they were ashamed of their sin. Jesus said: ***"My people, Adam and Eve hid from Me because of the shame of their guilt in eating the forbidden fruit. But they could not hide from Me as you cannot hide your sins from Me. What you do in secret can still be seen. So, do everything in the light, because all sin will hurt My community. Pray, My children, to help your brothers and sisters in their problems. Do not shame them or make judgments, but give them good example by encouraging them to be cleansed in the graces of Confession."***

I could see many tables with white tablecloths as people were entering to take their seats. Jesus said: ***"My people, in order for you to enter My Heavenly Banquet, you must be purified with a proper wedding garment. It is during life that you must prepare your souls so it is beautiful in My sight. You cannot purify yourself. You must call on My love and My mercy to forgive your sins. When you love Me, you will strive to please Me in your actions. Give good example to those around you so they can know how to seek Me and be saved. When you have gathered up heavenly treasures and kept the faith, you will then be purified and able to enter My Banquet."***

I could look into the sky and a bright light appeared. Jesus said: ***"My people, you have had many signs in the skies to witness My End Days. These planet alignments are but one more example of My preparation. Your scientists have even noted this rare occurrence. As these signs increase in their sequence, you will have more indications that My coming again is not far off. Be prepared, My friends, since you know not the day of My return."***

I could see a bright light shining on some bishops wearing their miters. Jesus said: ***"My people, your bishops will be coming under more scrutiny as the schism is near to being implemented. Evil men have been planning this abomination for some time.***

This split in My Church is already evident as you are seeing signs of it all around you. Keep your faith in My pope son, John Paul II, for he is leading you down the proper road to Heaven. Do not deviate from My traditional teaching when this Antipope will satisfy many itching ears for change. My laws and commandments do not change. Hold your faith close to your heart and never give in to your own will."

I could see a carnival of activity indicating how many are spending their precious time. Jesus said: ***"My people, many souls are busying themselves with many activities. It is up to you to determine the priorities of your own actions. If you busy yourselves with the earthly things, but leave no time for prayer, then you let life pass you by without any spiritual gain. Grow in your spiritual life by spending more time in my service and united in My quiet love of your soul. Take time out of your busy schedules to focus on Me in little daily retreats. See how your spiritual life is growing or not and make the proper adjustments in your actions to follow My will."***

Friday, February 26, 1999:

After Communion, I could see a white part of the ground where Jesus was writing the sins of the accusers of the adulteress. Jesus said: ***"My people, how quick you are to concur in accusing your brother of crimes, while you have guilt in your own sins. At times you may be called to correct your friends, but avoid making judgments when you may not have all of the facts or evidence of wrongdoing. I asked those before Me who had no sin to cast the first stone. You all are sinners and in need of repentance. This Lent is a good time to consider correcting your own faults. When you want to correct others, you cannot be hypocrites in asking them to do something you also have violated. So, leave your gift at the altar and make amends with those you have wronged by your actions. Once you have confessed your sins, then you will be purified enough to receive Me in Holy Communion. Do not take Me in Communion while you are in mortal sin, lest you commit a sin of sacrilege. Once purified, you can receive Me into your heart, and you will appreciate My peace and love that will set you free of your bonds of sin."***

Later, at St. Martin's Church, Louisville, Kentucky, I could see a beautiful church with statues in it. Jesus said: ***"My people, it is good to keep your statues in the church. The children need role models in the saints to help them lead good spiritual lives in imitation of the saints' holiness. A church with bare walls sends the wrong message to the faithful, who are hungry for the faith, but they are not being fed. Many are seeking the sacred and reverence for holy objects. It is up to the pastors to lead their people closer to Me as they are responsible for their parishioners' souls. Reach out to their hearts so the love of My word may inspire their souls to follow My Will. I am always loving all of My children and I wait patiently for you to return My love by your own free will."***

Saturday, February 27, 1999:

At St. Louis Bertrand Church, Louisville, Kentucky, after Communion, I could see an old confessional in the back of a church. Jesus said: ***"My people, you are always doing things to preserve your earthly body. Many times by instinct you strive in the body to survive. In the same way your soul has an instinct for its survival as well. Your soul is alive in My grace, but it is dead in mortal sin. That is why Confession is the lifeblood of the soul, because it is the channel of My graces and the forgiveness of your sins. Everyone is a sinner and in need of repentance. You have beautiful priests around you, so take advantage of every opportunity to cleanse your souls of sin by coming to Me with a contrite heart in the person of the priest. Your soul is many times steeped in guilt from sin and your soul desires My peace and***

love. When you are forgiven in your sins, it lifts a great burden from your shoulders. This is why I beckon to you to come follow Me, since My burden is light. When you are in sin, you carry a larger burden of troubles than when you are relieved after Confession. My light burden is that you love Me and follow My Commandments. This is a yoke of delight, for following Me will lead you to Heaven where your soul will find eternal rest.”

Later, at St. Martin’s Adoration, Louisville, Kentucky, I could see the ball of the New Years Celebration in New York City fall and break into many pieces. Jesus said: ***“My people, as the time of your computer problems draws closer to 2000, you will see many horror stories that could cause a massive chaos. The weakest link or where these problems have not been corrected, will cause a domino effect shutting down your power, your communications, and finally your means to transport food. Those who have reserves of food and fuel will be the only ones assured of eating. But when looting and searching for food begins, there will be few safe places to go. You will see the Antichrist manipulate food and money shortages to try and force people to take the Mark of the Beast. Refuse the Mark of the Beast at all costs and only worship Me. When men search for food with guns and when John Paul II leaves Rome, this is your indication to go into hiding to protect yourself from the influence of the Antipope and the Antichrist. Rely on Me for the grace to bring you through this tribulation. This is another expression of how your technology will bring about your downfall.”***

Sunday, February 28, 1999:

At St. Gabriel’s Church, Louisville, Kentucky, after Communion, I could see Jesus looking over the people at a Mass. Jesus said: ***“My people, I showed My apostles My glorified body so they would understand the beauty of My Resurrection. It was to give them hope before they received the Holy Spirit. This vision I am showing My people is one of My protection where I will be watching out for your souls in preparation for the tribulation. I am giving you hope in My word of comfort, so you can be protected as I did My apostles. A day is coming soon when I will cleanse the earth of evil and then I will recreate the earth and bring My faithful***

into My Era of Peace. So, come to Me in My sacraments and carry your sacramentals so you will be strengthened to endure this trial. Satan and the Antichrist will try to steal souls from Me, but you will be given the strength in My grace to resist Satan's temptations. Trust in Me and My love and you will receive your reward both on earth and in Heaven."

Monday, March 1, 1999:

After Communion, I could see a red floor and there were massive amounts of bugs from an infestation. Jesus said: ***"My people, a time is coming when your storms and droughts will upset the balance of nature, and there will be many unusual infestations of various insects and bugs. You have been chastised with weather disasters and earthquakes. Soon, your chastisements will include diseases and hordes of pests that will attack your food. Again, these events will test your resolve as your possessions will be threatened. Pray, My children, this Lent and repent of your sins while you have the grace of time. If there is not enough prayer to balance your sins, your chastisements could grow worse. It is man's own destruction of his environment that is causing these insect displacements. Much of your world reflects the effects of your evil actions."***

Later, at Adoration I saw someone emerging from the waters of Baptism. Jesus said: ***"My people, during Lent your catechumens are being prepared for their entry into the faith by Baptism. It is the waters of this sacrament that wash away your sins, making these souls into new faithful ready to accept Me into their lives. Even if you should fall into sin again, I have given you My Sacrament of Reconciliation to replenish your souls. By your contrite hearts seeking forgiveness, you can always be purified over and over with no excuse for not being in My graces. It is only the lazy souls who are too weak to come to Confession and those who refuse to seek My forgiveness, that will have difficulty entering Heaven. I have given you free will to accept Me into your lives or to reject Me. I will allow your choice, but you must accept the consequences. I knock on the doors of every soul to let Me into their hearts. Please open the door to Me, so I can arouse your love for Me. Once you love Me, there will be no end to the joy I will share with you."***

Tuesday, March 2, 1999:

After Communion, I could see a cobra snake about to strike. Jesus said: ***"My people, Satan is about to strike you with his evil plans, because his time is running out. The current crisis with***

your computer failures is about to get more serious. As people become more threatened to have enough food and fuel, shortages will develop quickly. I have warned you in advance to store food, water, and fuel up to the time of the Antichrist's appearance. The problem will occur when people are without their necessities. You can share your food with others and I will multiply what you have for others. It is those who begin to panic and start to steal and loot for their own needs that will cause trouble. It is the instinct of self-preservation that will cause massive riots and displacements all over the world. Money will no longer mean anything without a proper distribution means. It is for this reason that you may have to prepare to leave for safe places as these riots start. The powers in place are behind not fixing your problems sooner. They have known for a long time the results of their inactivity to fix your computers. This will give those looking to control the world the best opportunity to cause chaos for their takeover. Be prepared with your food, but also be prepared to leave at a short notice. Pray, My people, for My help and strength during this trial. Events are moving quickly to their completion."

Later, at Adoration, I could see a new coin encased in a small window in a church. Jesus said: ***"My people, you are seeing a new money system that will soon come about. It will require having the Mark of the Beast to make any transaction. It is the image of the Beast on this coin that everyone will worship. This will mean that your current money system will collapse with no value given, unless one takes the chip in the hand. Your electronic devices will have to be changed for this new system to work. Your possessions will indeed be stripped from you, since My faithful will not accept the Mark of the Beast. As the evil agents of the Antichrist seek to place this Mark of the Beast on everyone, you will have to go into hiding from the influence of the Antichrist. Those caught refusing this Mark will be imprisoned. Some will be martyred, while others will be tortured and made slaves of these evil masters. Have faith and hope in My help when I will lead you away from these evil people. My angels will be with you to provide for your needs and your protection. You will find My protection at My refuges away from the cities. After a short reign of the Anti-***

christ, I will triumph over all of the evil people and evil spirits, who will all be cast into Hell. My faithful I will then raise up in My Era of Peace. Be patient for a brief time, before I crush your enemies with My justice. My mercy will be among My faithful as you will enjoy My peace and love even amidst this evil. Keep focused on Me and your souls will be saved."

Wednesday, March 3, 1999:

After Communion, I could see the upper structure of an A-frame church. Jesus said: ***"My people, I am asking you to build up My Church. The structure of the church is important, but it is more important to build up the people in My Mystical Body. Reach out to My lost souls who have drifted away from the practice of their faith. Also, reach out to those souls of other faiths or souls who have not heard My Word. You can be My missionaries of love to join souls in My love, so they can share in My sacraments. Your time for saving souls grows short, and many could be lost if they are not invited to My Banquet. Saving souls has a price, but it is the most rewarding work you can do for Me. By your example and prayers, you can be a witness to others of My love in your hearts. Your sharing of My spirit can enlighten other souls to change their way of life. Helping souls takes a lot of effort and it is an ongoing work. Be persistent in your quest for souls and your reward will be great in Heaven."***

Later, at Adoration, I could see a comfortable easy chair with a light shining on it. Jesus said: ***"My people, I have been giving you warning messages to prepare you both spiritually and physically for the coming trial. I have asked you to prepare many sacramentals for the time when they will no longer be available. I have asked you to store food, water, and fuel. All of these warnings are to give you enough time to get ready for this time of chaos that the Antichrist will use to take over. So, do not get lazy and complacent in your current comforts. Get up and prepare by not depending on someone else. Follow My instructions and you will be prepared for the first stage of your shortages. You will know the time when it will not be safe to stay in your cities. You need to have a plan for a quick evacuation as your year draws to an end. Call on My help in this crisis and I will guide you in what***

to do. In all you do, remain peaceful and confident in My love. Be loving of your neighbor and do not let your body mislead your love of Me. In all of these trials I will shelter your souls. Remember that your spiritual life is the most important and not to threaten any of your neighbors. A time of chaos is coming, but have no fear because I am at your side."

Thursday, March 4, 1999:

At the prayer group at our house (due to the snow storm) I could see a dove representing the Holy Spirit. The Holy Spirit said: ***"I am the Spirit of Love and I come to console you and protect your souls in your trials. Call on Me and I will empower you to struggle through even the tribulation. I love you always and I am eager to share My gifts with you. You must seek Me in love to help you and I will grace you with all of your spiritual needs. Trust in My power and you will be saved."***

I could see a picture of someone graduating with a cap and gown. Jesus said: ***"My people, you all are being tested in this life and no one has an easy life. Some may have more severe testing, especially during the tribulation. Think of this life as your preparation to graduate into a heavenly life. Your transition into the next life is your graduation. When you are brought to Heaven, you will be resurrected one day with your glorified body. This will be your seal of perfection that you have received your diploma of eternal life with Me."***

I could see some trees and they sensed the destruction that was coming from man. Jesus said: ***"My people, you have brought evil ways to this world and now your evil has even affected your environment. Many of your chemicals that you have made are polluting your environment and are killing your plants and animals. I will have to recreate the earth again because of all of your destruction and imperfections. Seek to do things that are keeping nature pure and following My Will."***

I could see someone reading a book. Jesus said: ***"My people, many beautiful understandings have been captured in books. Those books that bring you closer in your love for Me are even more special. Take time this Lent to do some extra spiritual reading that will give you some food for thought in bettering your***

life. Be willing to take advice from others and you will be able to grow in your spirituality."

I could see a dark funnel cloud coming toward me. Jesus said: ***"My people, you are seeing destruction all over your country from snow storms, ice storms, high winds, floods, and tornadoes. I have told you that your possessions would be stripped from you and many have seen their property being destroyed. Your weather chastisements are a reaction in nature to the evil that you have brought on your land. Repent and I will relent of My justice upon you."***

I could see some large Egyptian statues. Jesus said: ***"My people, you have seen other civilizations and how they worshiped other gods. Without Me present to them, their worlds have destroyed themselves. They sought eternal life but only through the body. When you seek eternal life in the soul, it can only come through Me. Pray to follow My Will for you to be saved."***

I could see a woman being made up with make-up. Jesus said: ***"My people, many of you are vain and wish to portray yourselves as someone more than you are. Why are you not satisfied with your natural beauty? As you age, you are only fooling yourselves to change your appearance. Many can see through your attempts to look younger. Concentrate your thoughts on pleasing Me instead of pleasing others with your looks. I know all and you are not fooling Me about anything you do. Focus on having your soul look beautiful to Me and that will be enough for you."***

I could see oil gushing up through the ground. Jesus said: ***"My people, many think they would have instant riches to strike oil on their land. You have seen many uses come from your oil, but all of these will be cut off from you as your computer problems get worse. Your fuels for heating, transportation, and electricity have become a core part in your modern lives. You will be experiencing many shortages in these end times that will gradually lead to the chaos bringing on the peace of the Antichrist. Know that his time will come when mankind is looking for someone to save them from their disasters. But the Antichrist's peace will be turned into a dictatorship where he will reign briefly over the whole world. I will then bring My triumph over him and evil will be cleansed from the earth. I will restore the earth to its former beauty and My faithful will enjoy My Era of Peace."***

Friday, March 5, 1999:

After Communion, I could see some clouds moving in. Jesus said: ***"My people, your storm will be just a bump in the road, compared to those things you will witness in the coming tribulation. You will never be fully prepared, but make your best efforts both spiritually and physically. It is important that you keep your focus on Me in all that you will endure. By following My Will and seeking My help and that of your guardian angel, you will succeed in saving your souls. No matter how much you will be tested by Satan and the Antichrist, My faithful will be protected. Some may suffer martyrdom and persecution, but My faithful will be guarded against all evil. Have faith and hope in My protection and you will enjoy the beauty of the coming Era of Peace. Bear with this trial but a moment, and you will see the reward of your pain."***

Later, I could see a bright light going up to Heaven through the church. Jesus was standing there welcoming a soul. Jesus said: ***"My people, all funerals are a word of caution to all watching, that you keep yourself cleansed of sin. You never know when you will be called home. Once you die, there is no turning back. So, come to Me with good works in your hands, and offer up all of your sufferings to diminish your time in Purgatory. Remember to continue praying for your deceased relatives and never forget them. Your world here is short, so be ever prepared for your eternal journey. I will be there to bring you home one day at your resurrection. Be faithful and fight the good fight."***

Saturday, March 6, 1999:

At Epiphany Church, Sayre, Pennsylvania, after Communion, I could see a Mass being said in the crypt of the church. Jesus said: ***"My people, you should treasure every opportunity to go to Mass and share with Me in Holy Communion. At every Mass you give witness to a miracle of My changing the bread and wine into My Body and My Blood. There will come a day when it will be difficult to find a priest to say Mass. The priests will be banned from the churches during the tribulation, so there will only be underground Masses at that time. But I will not leave you alone. As you call on Me in Spiritual Communion, I will have your angels***

give you my heavenly manna, so you will always have My Real Presence among you. This will require full trust in Me to leave your things behind and let My angels lead you to My safe havens. As you were fully resigned to losing your clothes on your trip, that is the same commitment I am looking for in My faithful during the tribulation. This full trust will mean giving yourself completely to following My will. You will not bear the strain of the evil ones, unless you seek My help and that of your guardian angel. Trust and hope in My protection and I will provide for all of your needs."

Later, at St. Francis of Assisi Church, Mildred, Pennsylvania, I could see myself traveling down a road through the woods. Jesus said: ***"My people, each person travels along the road of their life with a plan that I have made specifically for that soul. By your Baptism you are set on the road to Heaven, but you are detoured by the many allurements of the world. I have given you the living water of My grace in the Sacrament of Reconciliation. As you come to Me in Confession to express your sorrow for your sins, you are cleansed again of the sins on your soul. When you are absolved of your sins, you are then set back on your road to Heaven. You need to pray for discernment and knowledge of the understanding of your sins, so you will know when you are deviating from My plan for you. It is eternal life that your soul is constantly seeking, so it can find its rest in My peace. Keep ever focused on Me and you will find your eternal reward in Heaven."***

Sunday, March 7, 1999:

At St. Basil's Church, Dushore, Pennsylvania, after Communion, I could see some spirits graduating to their eternal life in heaven. Jesus said: ***"My people, I love you so much and I call you to follow Me in life as I called My apostles. Those that accept Me as Lord of their lives and seek the forgiveness of their sins are those who have washed their robes. My faithful in life hear My voice and follow Me as My sheep into My sheepfold. I am showing you those worthy faithful that are rising to Heaven in their spirits. This is only a life of sorrows and suffering here on earth. By your faithful endurance, you also can graduate to your eternal reward in Heaven. I call everyone to be a saint in My love and***

with My help. Continue to aspire to your perfection through Me and one day, My angel will escort you to your place I have prepared for you in Heaven."

Later, at St. Ann's Adoration, Hampton, New Jersey, I could see a crucifix of Jesus being carried among the people. Jesus said: ***"My people, you do not know how much I long to be among you in My Real Presence. When you come to Me in Adoration, I share My abundant graces with those willing to spend some time with Me. The more you give Me thanks and Adoration, the closer I am to your hearts. My love and peace are like a magnet that draws your souls to visit Me. I am asking My priests and laity to promote My Adoration in whatever hours you can. I am the one you should be looking to for strength in these coming trials. Where I am exposed for your worship, these areas are blessed with My gifts. Continue to come to Me and share your daily troubles. Give your burdens over to Me, and I will lighten your load. My Real Presence is to be praised and honored for as long as possible until the tribulation arrives. Even during that time, you can call on Me for Spiritual Communion, and I will allow My angels to bring you My heavenly manna. Have no fear, My children, and continue to seek My help in all that you do."***

Monday, March 8, 1999:

At St. Ann's Church, Hampton, New Jersey, after Communion, I could see a quinsy hut with an altar and a crucifix was lying on the ground. I then saw a pure white room for an individual. Jesus said: ***"My people, I am showing you My underground church that I will give strength to survive despite the evil efforts of the Antichrist. Pray for My help and that of your guardian angel during your time of the trial. You will see the Antichrist grow quickly in power over the whole world. Many will even worship him as a god. My Church will seem defeated for a moment, but have no fear, since the evil one will have his day in the sun. I will never abandon you, but you will suffer severe persecution for a time. Just as the Antichrist will come to full power throughout the whole world, I will smite him as he will fall from power. His kingdom will fall from within as quickly as he came to power. My final chastisement will then strike the final blow that will be his***

utter defeat. I will lead My angels to victory in the final Battle of Armageddon. Then you will see My glory reign as all the evil people and evil spirits will be chained in Hell. I will then raise up My people as I recreate the world again. My faithful will then share My reward in My Era of Peace. Rejoice, My people, for as you see these things begin, you will know that Satan's power will soon be vanquished."

Tuesday, March 9, 1999:

After Communion, I could see someone gritting his teeth in anger at an injustice. Jesus said: ***"My people, many times people offend you or cause you harm in some way. Your immediate response sometimes draws you into anger or rage over your injustice. Your earthly inclination is to punish this person by making restitution for your loss or harm. My friends, when someone causes you harm or inconvenience, wait quietly for a few moments to hold back your earthly impulse. In that quick moment of thought, answer each instance as I would with compassion and forgiveness. Do not force the issue, but make your comments of how you were wronged and give the other person a chance to explain your hurt. Allow them a chance to make any damage right and tell them that you forgive them from your heart. Do not hold grudges or look to get even by your own means. Come to each situation in a loving way to compromise your differences. If it is necessary, call in another arbiter in your situation, giving the judgment up to Me or some legal authority. It is much better for you to forgive in minutes that to hold a grudge for years. I love you unconditionally, even despite all of your sins. You should always forgive your neighbor in a like manner and you will be rewarded in Heaven."***

Later, at Adoration, I could see a man giving directions with his hands as a ruler. Jesus said: ***"My people, I am showing you to be watchful of your leaders both politically and spiritually. Watch more what they do than what they say, because words can be deceiving. There are more corrupt leaders in your national government than in your local government. The more money that controls these leaders, the more they will be swayed by their benefactors. Discern your leaders' views on the moral issues of the***

day and you will know where they stand. Pray for your government leaders and your bishops and priests. Your leaders are responsible for building up the faithful. If they do not support traditional values according to My Ten Commandments, then they are doing a disservice for their people. I hold all of your leaders accountable for their actions. Your leaders are responsible for holding the peace and for any crimes or corruption at the higher levels. It is My peace that I will give at My triumph that will supercede your earthly rulers. All of the evil, corrupt leaders will be then cast into Hell and all life will be according to My Will at My Era of Peace. Seek My leadership for one you can trust and for your Lord who loves you always."

Wednesday, March 10, 1999:

After Communion, I could see several eyes looking at me. Jesus said: ***"My people, you should be more vigilant in your behavior, because many eyes are watching your every action. So, guard your tongue from swearing over every little inconvenience. Do not go into rages of anger where others can see you. Look to help others in need instead of ignoring them. You should show a loving attitude in all you do, so that you are a good example of Christian living. By your following My Commandments in front of everyone, you are witnessing more by your actions than all of your words. Bringing souls to Me requires that you are not hypocrites of the faith you believe in. You must live your faith in your actions, if you want others to believe in Me. It is not just going to church that will save you, but it is a life commitment to follow My Will."***

Later, at Adoration, I could see a man in a dark silhouette calling on a phone. Jesus said: ***"My people, there are many people taking down information on each of you. Information on your spending habits, your telephone calls, and even your movements can be monitored, if you are on the wrong lists. As time draws closer to the time of tribulation, you should be a little wary of your personal information. Your preparations of food and shelter will be needed, especially without the Mark of the Beast. As your shortages of necessities becomes more acute, you will need to be ready to leave on short notice. You will need your***

Sacramentals, some bedding, and warm clothes for your flight to safety. Be not afraid what the evil ones can do, but trust in My protection. You will have to undergo a persecution for My Name's sake and some may even face the possibility of martyrdom. Pray, My people, for My strength in these days, where you will be thoroughly tested."

Thursday, March 11, 1999:

After Communion, I could see a dead body being floated down a river on a raft by several people in the water. Jesus said: *"My people, I am showing you this dead body floating in the river to symbolize your passing into eternity. The river is endlessly flowing water to indicate your immortality. You will be greeted by those whom you know and have gone to Heaven. These are the souls assisting you on the raft. All souls must face a fork in this river that determines your destination by My judgment of your soul. At the point of your death, you have no control of where you will be sent. Those who have made restitution for their sins will be led to My glory in Heaven. Those who have accepted Me, but need purification of their sins, will suffer for a time in Purgatory and join Me later in Heaven. Those who have rejected Me even to their death and did not seek forgiveness of their sins will be condemned to an eternity in Hell. My mercy abounds for the least repentant sinner, but My justice lies in wait for those totally defiant of My love."*

Later, at the prayer group, I could see people smoking drugs and other means of taking drugs. Jesus said: *"My people, money is the evil behind drugs, and some leaders in high places are profiting from drug sales to addicts. Your drug culture is destroying many lives and it creates more crimes of theft and murder. All of the attempts to stop drugs have not succeeded because there is too much corruption in your government. Pray for the young people not to get involved with drugs and pray for the cure of those on drugs."*

I could see a few people in a large stadium. Jesus said: *"My people, beware of the one who claims himself to be Me. The Antichrist will cause many to follow him as a man of peace to save the world from the chaos and turmoil that will come. You are so*

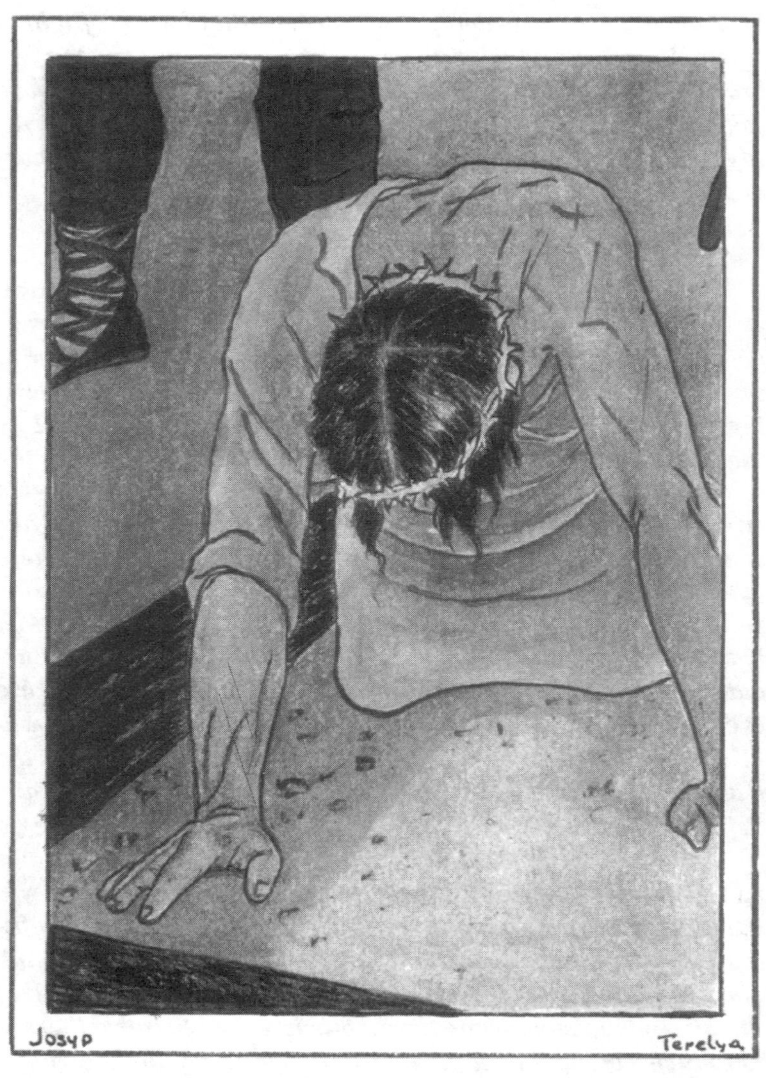

taken up with your gains in the stock market, that these greedy people will follow anyone helping them to save their money. Do not take the Mark of the Beast and do not listen to those wanting you to worship anyone else but Me."

I could see the streets of the Old City of Jerusalem where Jesus walked with many crosses in place. Jesus said: ***"My people, I call***

on you to remember My passion and suffering at the hands of My own people. Those who believe in My Name find themselves being persecuted for going against the pleasures and comforts of the world. The worldly cannot understand that your spiritual life transcends your physical life. They think My faithful are fools to concern themselves with the life after death. Keep your focus on following My Will and My Commandments and you will find a joy beyond anything that can be found on earth."

I could see Jesus praying in His agony in the garden. Jesus said: ***"My people, I ask you to pray with Me in your Lenten devotions as I asked My apostles to watch one hour with Me. If you could pray one hour each day with Me, your Lent would be very profitable to your soul. It is your persistence in your prayer life that is most important. Just as My apostles wanted to sleep, many good intentions of My faithful are lost because they are being spiritually lazy. Take up your prayer books and renew your spirit in being steadfast to your Lenten resolutions."***

I could see a church inside and many candles were lying on the ground. Jesus said: ***"My people, pray for your priests that they will not grow lax in their prayers and devotions to me. Without prayer it is hard to keep your link in My love. The priests are the ones to inspire you with improving your spiritual lives during Lent. By encouraging the 'stations of the cross' and Confession, the faithful can grow in their faith. Support and pray for your priests so they are encouraged by your positive response to My love. I open My arms to you to grow closer in your love for My Sacred Heart."***

I could see a lantern of light at a lamppost. Jesus said: ***"My people, I am the Light of the World and I show you the way to your salvation. Listen to My words so they may direct you on your path to Heaven. See that My love reaches out as a beam of grace to all those seeking to be with Me. I will give you the rest that your soul is seeking. Give up your own will so I can lead you home by following My Divine Will."***

I could see many mounds of sand in the desert with a bright sun shining down. Jesus said: ***"My people, you are tested with many sufferings in life that everyone must bear patiently. Your recent storms have brought many difficulties to bear. Have faith*** *in My help and do not despair with life's trials. Every test you face, becomes another question of how much you love Me. When you call on My blessings, I will be there to support you. No matter how impossible your trial may be, I will bring you through each experience with a gain in your confidence of My presence in your lives. Seek me in My sacraments and I will bring a heavenly rest to your soul. I love you so much and I seek your love in return. You will be rewarded for putting up with your trials, as long as your faith is at the center of your life."*

Friday, March 12, 1999:

After Communion, I could see angels holding and blowing their trumpets. Jesus said: ***"My people, My angels have already marked those to be saved of My faithful. Those who will convert after My Warning have yet to be marked. That is why these souls, that you can evangelize, will have their last chance by My mercy. You are approaching the time when I will have My angels blow their trumpets to announce the coming plagues. All of the events leading up to the time of the Antichrist are about to proceed. There will be much suffering at first by My faithful, who will be persecuted. My faithful will be going to My refuges for protection with My angels. After the Antichrist comes to full power, all of his demons and the evil people will suffer their own living Hell on earth from the plagues announced by My angels' trumpets. Those who reject Me will envy the dead, for their suffering will have no end. Come to Me now, while you are still able to repent, for the unrepentant sinner will have much to suffer."***

Later, at St. Stanislaus Kostka Church, Woonsocket, R.I., after Communion, I could see a censer, a monstrance and kneelers. Jesus said: ***"My people, you have a rich treasure in your Catholic traditions. I have given you My very self in My Eucharistic Presence. It is My Real Presence that you are adoring and giving praise. Cast your eyes on My Consecrated Host and give Me all of your daily troubles. When you give yourself over to My Will, I will lead you through life with a peace that will keep you at ease even through the most difficult of trials. Keep your faith in Me and keep your focus on following My ways and you will not be far from My kingdom. I love you so much and I treasure My*** *precious moments with each soul after receiving Me in Holy Communion. I am present for you so you can seek Me in prayer and love. By your love of Me and your neighbor, you can be working to perfect your spiritual life. Do not despair in your sins or your troubles, but seek Me in Confession to cleanse your souls. When you receive My Host worthily, you will be as fulfilled as you can be on this earth, as My peace will give rest to your soul."*

Saturday, March 13, 1999:

At St. Stanislaus Kostka Church, Woonsocket, R.I., after Communion, I could see a shadow of myself. Jesus said: ***"My people, as you see your shadow walking with you, you also have your spirit walking in your body. In order to direct yourself to Heaven, you must appreciate how important it is to form a proper conscience to decide between right and wrong. I have given you My Commandments as a model for life in loving your God and your neighbor as yourself. I have given you My revelation in Scripture, so you have My words on how to imitate My life. But you must take upon yourself a measure of how to know right from wrong. Without this right conscience, it will be difficult to know what offends Me and how to follow My Will. Listen to My priests and My pope how to understand the evils of your day. When you focus your life to please Me, look into your life how to correct your sins. See yourself as a sinner looking to improve, instead of like the Pharisee who seeks only pride in his actions. Love is the basis of life. If you follow My love and not your own will, My Will will direct you in every way to gain Heaven. Seek to cleanse your sins frequently in Confession and study My life as a model to form your consciences properly. You are living in an age of apostasy, but I give you a proper faith for those who believe, so you can follow in My steps to Calvary and to Heaven."***

Later, at St. Stanislaus Kostka Church, Woonsocket, R.I., I could see someone kissing the foot of the altar and discarding a sword. Jesus said: ***"My people, I ask you to give Me all the praise and the glory and to reject taking up the sword in your defense. I have told St. Peter to put away the sword as I am telling you the same. It is enough for you to give your life over to My service. Do not be caught up in fighting over land and possessions. These are the*** *ways of the evil one to take up arms. Stop your fighting and forgive your persecutors. When you follow My Will, I do not ask you to kill. Instead I ask you to preserve life in all of its forms. I am the one to make judgments and I am the one to call souls home to Me in My time. Learn to love one another and go the extra mile to be peacemakers. You are too quick to cause wars for gain in profit. Do not follow the evil ones who encourage injustices and want to control the world. Fame and fortune in this world are not your goals. Instead seek only to be with Me in Heaven by following My Will. Pray for My peace that will soon reign over the earth."*

Sunday, March 14, 1999:

At St. Stanislaus Kostka Church, Woonsocket, R.I., after Communion, I could see an ornate altar with the Blessed Sacrament in Adoration in the monstrance. Jesus said: ***"My people, your soul is thirsting for your living God. My Real Presence is drawing you to Me, because I am the only one who can give rest to your soul. When you come before Me, you have peace and love surround you. I love you so much that I died to redeem you from your sins. I call on everyone of My followers to open your hearts to receive Me, Body and Blood, through My Eucharist. It is My sacrament that will bestow My grace and mercy among you. By following My Will in My Commandments, you will be led by My love to join Me in Heaven. Remain faithful to My calling and you will see your eternal reward in Heaven."***

Monday, March 15, 1999:

After Communion, I could see gold and white robes of a large celebration when the Antipope will be elected. Jesus said: ***"My people, your events are moving quickly to their completion. The time of a new pope being installed is coming soon. It will be at this same time that you will see My pope son, John Paul II, being exiled. Once this evil pope takes over, he will quickly align himself with the world politics. He will establish new church laws that will violate My old traditions. He will make a mockery out of My beliefs of the faith. His ultimate insult to Me will be to encourage My faithful to believe in and worship the Antichrist. In search of his own power as a papal state, he will join a world*** *alliance that serves the Antichrist. Do not follow this evil pope, who will misguide people to sin. His false decrees are not supported by the Holy Spirit and their evil will be made known to My elect, so they will not follow these evil ways. Test this evil pope by discernment and the fruit of his deeds. A bad tree cannot bring forth good fruit, nor can a good tree bear bad fruit."*

Later, I could see many beautiful trees in the forest. Jesus said: *"My people, you are very comfortable in your homes with heat, light, food and water. What are you to do when it comes time to leave the comfort of your homes in exchange for an unknown hiding place at a refuge? My pope son will leave soon, so you have to plan what you will do. There will come a time before martial law is declared, that the Antichrist's agents will seek out those who will be against the New World Order. They will come by stealth in the night to take any religious leaders or other dissidents away to the death camps. This is why I have told you to go into hiding before the Antichrist can carry out his secret plans. You will need full trust that I will lead you to safe havens and supply you with all of your needs. This test of evil will have a short reign, but you will have to call on My help to bring you through this time. If you do not leave soon enough, you could risk being killed, tortured, or enslaved at the detention centers. Pray for discernment and strength to have My angels lead you to your place of protection. Have no fear, but only trust in My Word."*

Tuesday, March 16, 1999:

After Communion, I could see a sack of food and sacramentals ready for hiding. Jesus said: *"My people, I have brought you through all of life's trials to this point. Why should you have any fear that I will not watch over you in the most difficult tribulation to come? Have your food and sacramentals packed and ready to leave when the time comes of when I told you to leave. Do not be fearful of the plans of the evil one. Some will be martyred for their faith, but those, who follow My direction to My refuges, will be protected. Do not worry about the physical details. It is enough that you are focused on saving your souls. There will be difficult testing for My faithful, but the suffering of the unfaithful will be far worse. Be grateful that I am cleansing the earth at this time,*

so the evil one will no longer steal souls from Me. You are all called to be with Me in Heaven. Leave the time and the circumstances to Me and you will be provided for."

Later, I could see a monstrance with the Host and the glass on the monstrance was shattered. Jesus said: ***"My people, are ye of little faith? When I died on the cross, I bled real blood. I died that your sins may be forgiven. I have given you My real Body and Blood under the appearances of bread and wine at every Mass during the Consecration. Yet many refuse to believe in My Real Presence. The devil tries to belittle My Presence, because he knows the power of the Consecrated Host. The devil continues to take away all sense of the sacred in any way he can get man to disbelieve. It is true faith that gives witness that I am present in the Host and this makes your churches holy. The miracles of My Eucharist in bleeding Hosts or flesh give witness in miracles to My Real Presence. There are many doubting Thomases who do not believe in My Real Presence. Even St. Thomas believed in My Resurrection when he felt My side and the nail marks in My hands. But you see My bleeding Hosts and persist in your unbelief. Happy are those who have not seen Me and still they believe. Those who do not testify to My Real Presence in the Eucharist have a faith that is weak indeed. I love you, My people, and I will remain with you to the end of this age through My Presence in My Consecrated Hosts."***

Wednesday, March 17, 1999: (St. Patrick's Day)

After Communion, I could see a cloth table and people were seating themselves. Jesus said: ***"My people, every day I call you to My Eucharistic table at the Mass. You all are eager to come to the supper table to feed your bodies. You should be even more eager to feed your soul with My heavenly manna. The food of Myself, that I offer you, is everlasting, because I nourish your spirit with My graces and I strengthen you in your battle against sin. You need to be aware of the threats of sin to your spiritual life. Your soul will live on forever and you should take more care of your eternal destiny. By focusing your life on Me and following My Will, you will be on the right road to Heaven. Even if you falter, My cleansing graces at Confession await your return to***

My favor. Seek to love Me and your neighbor every day and do not be selfish with your time and your treasure. Those who listen to My Word and follow Me will be received at My heavenly banquet forever."

Later, at Adoration, I could see a bridge between two churches. Jesus said: *"My people, a time is coming when many churches will all be joined in a One World religion. The Antipope, who will replace Pope John Paul II, will make accommodations to join all religions as one. Many traditions of My Church will be compromised under the guise of unity. Unifying the churches will be one more step by the Masons toward One World control. This One World religion will then allow the Antichrist an opportunity to have everyone worship him as a world ruler. Do not follow either the Antichrist or this Antipope, who will be trying to deceive the people not to have allegiance to Me only. You will see how the New Age movement will draw innocent people into following this One World religion. Do not be fooled, but continue to remain faithful to Me and not these false witnesses."*

Thursday, March 18, 1999:

After Communion, I could see soldiers marching in ranks. They were dressed in gold and a heavenly cloud covered their faces. Jesus said: *"My people, I am showing this array of soldiers so you can see my angels assembling for the Battle of Armageddon. I will provide you My warriors to fight your battles against Satan and his demons. A time is coming when Satan will be defeated and all of his forces and himself will be chained in Hell by My angels. The last chastisement will bring down a black curtain on all of the earth. All of the evil spirits and evil people will be wiped from the face of the earth in My victorious triumph. Fear not the evil ones, when you have Me at your side fighting your battles. There will be a time of testing and uncertainty during the tribulation, but by remaining faithful to Me, you will have no worries. Trust in My miraculous help in those days and I will share My reward with you in Heaven and on earth."*

Later, at the prayer group, I could see someone praying on a kneeler in church. Jesus said: *"My people, there are many of My children suffering in pain. It is difficult to endure pain, but re-*

member to offer it up for your sins and those of others. Some have been graced with cures, while others must bear the limit of their tolerance of pain. Pray for those in pain for relief of their pain and to comfort them. Show your concern for the sick, even if they are incurable or terminal. They look for you to remember them in their need and do not ignore them. Every soul seeks to be loved and recognized."

I could see a man wearing dark glasses and his appearance was very secretive. Jesus said: ***"My people, there are many secretive organizations working with stealth behind the scenes. Your politicians and money people are selling out your rights on their way to world control. Power and fortune drive many of your leaders. Remember that I promised you that I would humble the wise of the world and exult the lowly. Concentrate your priorities on heavenly riches, for earthly fame and riches are fleeting."***

I could see a cloudy image of a new Easter candle. Jesus said: ***"My people, Holy Week is not far off in your Lenten devotions. Prepare yourself for this Easter celebration by going to Confession. Let My life come into those souls that have been darkened by sin. It is not just enough to come to church on Easter. You must give witness to the forgiveness of your sins. Make this suggestion to your own family members and friends, so Easter will lift up their spirits in My light. Love needs to be a part of your life at all times, even when you fall on hard times. It is not painful to smile, so struggle to have a good disposition, even amidst your trials."***

I could see St. Joseph and some wooden figures. St. Joseph said: ***"My children, I was entrusted with a heavy responsibility in caring for Jesus and Mary. It is not easy to provide for a family even in your own day. You need to put up with a daily struggle for food and shelter. By working with Jesus in your labors and following His life, you will succeed. Imitate My life as well in being humble, yet dedicated to providing a living for your families. Be satisfied with the necessities of life without being envious or over ambitious for wealth. Dedicate your lives to love of God and neighbor and Jesus will see to your needs."***

I could see someone holding out their hands to greet me and St. Patrick came. St. Patrick said: ***"My dear son, I am happy to see you will be visiting Ireland once again. You have warmed my***

heart to give me attention in your prayers and to seek out places where I worked. It is good to know of your roots and understand how many of your traits were passed down to you. It is your free will that moves to form your consciences. Follow the Trinity in directing your life and you will find your way to Heaven."

I could see an altar for sacrifice with fire raging on it. Jesus said: ***"My people, I have told you that it is mercy I desire most over burnt offerings. In the days of the Old Testament, a sacrifice was made to give thanks for a person's blessings. Sacrifice was also a means of giving honor to Me and for the atonement for sin. As I am the Lamb who was sacrificed on Calvary, walk with Me in your own sufferings to your own Calvary. I have redeemed your souls through My Crucifixion. Now, you can take advantage of My gift of life by coming to Me in Confession with a contrite heart. Use the sacraments I have given you, so one day you may be resurrected as well."***

I could see someone at the workplace doing their job. Jesus said: ***"My people, your work can be a means to your salvation. With your hands and your mind you can use the talents you were given so that others may benefit from your labors. By your faith, you can give good example to those workers around you. By your witness and kind deeds, you can even lead souls back to Me. So, live a life of dedication to your heavenly goal by consecrating everything you do to Me. I will see your intentions in your heart and reward you for your good deeds. Love each other by leading Christian lives of good example."***

Friday, March 19, 1999: (St. Joseph's Day)

After Communion, I could see a large Host on a wall contrasted to a large hammer and sickle on another wall. Jesus said: ***"My people, many have seen symbols of the United Nations and Russia in some great halls, but I am showing you My Host as the answer to man's peace. My peace and love are far more perfect than man's peace. Your idea of peace is no war or forcing nations by military means to the peace table. My peace does not tolerate any fighting and promotes love of everyone. If everyone loved their neighbor more, there would be no fighting. So, do not be satisfied with man's peace. Instead, pray that My peace will be***

invoked over the whole world. It is only through love that this goal will be achieved. Remove your selfish desires from your heart and replace it with My love."

Saturday, March 20, 1999:

At Mom's place after Communion, I could look out a window and I saw the children being drawn to Jesus. I then saw Jesus lift a lamb on His shoulder. Jesus said: ***"My people, you know I love you with an infinite and unconditional love. If only one of you sinned against Me, I would still have died for that one lost sheep. Look on My coming to the earth as a fulfillment of My promise to redeem all of mankind. By Adam's sin, all were kept from entering into Heaven. Now, by My death, Heaven's Gates have been opened, because I have made atonement for all of your sins. You, My faithful, I call on to seek Me in your forgiveness of your sins. You have seen Me stripped of My clothes, insulted, persecuted, and crucified. I have done this also as an example to you. I call you as little children in blind faith to follow Me. Just as I was a willing Lamb of God led to the slaughter, you must suffer for My Name's sake. I have stripped you of many of your earthly possessions, so be willing to resign yourself to giving them up. Even for some, I will call on you to give up your most prized possession, that is your very life in martyrdom. In such a gift to Me, you would receive an instant heavenly reward. Do not be afraid to suffer for Me, but be willing in your heart to give everything that is yours over to Me, then I will know in your heart how much you love Me."***

Sunday, March 21, 1999:

At St. Michael's Norbetine Abbey, Orange County, California, after Communion, I could see a solitary dark chair with a bright light on it. Then a darkness came over the chair. Jesus said: ***"My people, I am showing you a symbol of life while you walk in My light. As the veil of death comes over the body, there is a loss of the life breath and My light is taken away. I am the Resurrection and the life. Whoever is faithful, has My light among them. This is a gift of faith you should not take lightly. It is only through Me that you can have salvation. All life comes through Me and I am the judge of your soul when you die. Prepare through life for the***

day when you will meet your Master. For you will have to make an accounting for all of your actions. I am merciful and understanding, but you must accept Me into your heart, if you are ever to follow My light. I call every soul to walk in My light of faith. Those souls that refuse to love Me and refuse to accept Me into their lives are to be condemned forever in the darkness. I love you, My people, so seek My light where I hold My arms out to receive you. Those who love Me and love their neighbor will enjoy life eternal in My presence with all of my saints and angels. Follow My light and one day I will resurrect your soul into eternal life with Me."

Later, at St. Christopher's Adoration, Irvindale, California, I could see a white statue of Our Lady of Fatima in a beautiful church. Jesus said: ***"My people, the prophecies of Fatima are about to come true. If there is not enough prayer, several nations could be annihilated before the end of this century. This is in conjunction with the message I gave you that if there were not enough prayers said, weapons of mass destruction could be used. Pray, My people, as you never have prayed before. Pray while you still have time to sway the balance of evil. Satan and his demons want to destroy man. He will test you dearly, but I still give you free will to choose to reverse the path your country is headed. My justice is about to rain down on the earth for all of its evil. Pray that My triumph comes before any further mass killing occurs. I want you to be on your knees praying in order to turn back this attempt by Satan. You have My mother's weapons in this battle, so use them now before it is too late."***

Monday, March 22, 1999:

At Adoration, I could see a sign post at the corner of two roads. Jesus said: ***"My people of America, you are coming to a crossroads when you will have to make a decision. You can go down the road of continuing to kill My babies and committing your sins of the flesh, or you can change your lives and follow Me. Through prayer and deed you can turn around your death culture. Stop killing innocent souls and refrain from your sins and I would hold back My justice. This time of Lent is your time to turn away from your ways of sin and purify your souls through My forgive-***

ness in Confession. Another crossroad is whether you will become involved in making war against the Serbs. It has been My desire for you to seek peace in a compromise and not at the point of a gun. It is not your place to interfere in another country's ongoing divisions. The Serbs are committing an injustice in killing their ethnic Albanians, but more killing is not the answer, nor are threats of further destruction. Continue to pray for your country's problems and sins, and to pray for peace in your world."

Tuesday, March 23, 1999:

I could see a priest dressed in purple vestments ready to distribute Holy Communion. Jesus said: ***"My people, I am calling you to receive Me in My Consecrated Host, so I can be with you in My Real Presence. Receive Me reverently as your Lord comes into your soul. Have your soul properly prepared to receive Me without any mortal sin. Many do not fully appreciate how great an honor it is to receive Me in My Eucharist. I love you, My dear children, and I long to be with you at every moment. As I love you, I call on you to love Me in return and thank Me for all I have done for you. It is through Me only that you can have eternal life. Do not worship anything else or anyone but Me. Only I am worthy of your worship, for I am Lord over everything. There is no excuse for not knowing of My existence. It is the desire to believe in Me that is more difficult for some. My warning will be an obvious alert to everyone of My existence and how I see their sins. I am giving you this mercy so everyone will know Me and have a reason for choosing to love Me. Without accepting Me as Savior and seeking the forgiveness of your sins, you cannot be saved. So come to Me in faith and believe that I am the gateway to Heaven for every soul."***

Later, I could see some helicopter blades circling and the helicopters were firing missiles at the tanks. Jesus said: ***"My people, be careful America, for what you are planning to do in Kosovo. Massive bombing again could draw other countries into a major conflict. If Russia and China involve their forces, you would be starting something that would be hard to finish. It is bad enough that you are spreading destruction, but now you are insulting Me both during the Christmas celebration and now in Passion Week.***

Here alone you can see the diabolic hand involved with this fighting. Pray that your leaders will hold back on such an involved bombing attack. More lives will be placed in jeopardy than all of those killed thus far. Peace is your only decision over a larger war. Your prayers are most needed at this hour."

Wednesday, March 24, 1999:

After Communion, I could look from the grass up into a sunlit sky and clouds were gathering on the horizon. Jesus said: ***"My people, all eyes are on the battlefield as you witness the lull before the storm. Once your attacks begin, there will be many questions as to where this will end. Without much of a plan, this move could well spread into a bigger war. Beware, My friends, that those who take up the sword, will see many killed as a result. These inner conflicts are never really solved by war, since this anger on each side will never end. Punishing Sadam in Iraq has only raised his resolve to fight. You will find the same in Kosovo with even the threat of nations coming to support the Serbs. You were warned of these consequences. Now, you may live to regret them. Wars cannot be fought without the loss of life. I ask you to continue praying for peace, so these leaders will stop their madness."***

Later, at Adoration, I could see the sun eclipsed by the moon. Jesus said: ***"My people, I have asked you to look to the skies for the signs of your End Times. The Warning is coming soon and there will be some celestial signs of its coming. This heavenly sign will be the same sign that I have told you about at the time of the Warning. There will be a darkness associated with this event. My faithful must have confidence in Me to protect you and to show you the way to Heaven. By having your souls cleansed at all times, you will be ready to receive Me in this experience. You are always more pleasing to My sight with your souls clean. It is also in your state of grace that you will be ready to receive Me in Holy Communion and in a state ready to come to Heaven at your death. Prepare for your warning when everyone will be fully aware of their sins."***

Thursday, March 25, 1999: (The Annunciation)

After Communion, I could see Mary in blue and white and she turned her face down and was weeping. Mary said: ***"My dear chil-***

dren, you are seeing now why I have appeared as a mother seeking peace for her children in Yugoslavia. My apparitions in Medjugorje have been to encourage prayer for peace, especially in this area that has ignited many wars. Satan has inspired evil men to direct the atrocities you have seen here in Serbia. There have been noble reasons given to stop this leader of Serbia from his ethnic cleansing, as you have put it. But more killing and destruction is not the answer for my Son, Jesus. Satan is trying to stir up a larger war and many of you do not see his objective in destroying as much of humanity as he can. You cannot have war in a vacuum. Such a war cannot help but affect their neighbors and other allied nations. Your leaders are confused in their selfish objectives that will only lead to the killing of innocent people. Pray, pray, pray for peace in this conflict which could only lead to a wider war. If enough prayer is not forthcoming, you could see the start of World War III."

Later, at the prayer group, I could see someone holding a scroll toward the people. Jesus said: ***"My people, I have given you My Commandments through Moses many years ago. This was the model I have given you to love your God and love your neighbor. When I came upon the earth, I gave you further example of My life to imitate. I never encouraged you to fight one another. Instead I told you that he, who lives by the sword, will die by the sword. A world without love will be a world without peace. Do not have anger against your neighbor, but learn to live with peaceful compromise."***

I could see many old weapons of war hanging in a museum. Jesus said: ***"My people, learn from history how futile it is to cause war against neighboring nations. Many have fought for many reasons in the past only to show their power. Many civilizations survived only by destroying their aggressive neighbors. Fighting for possessions and land is so fleeting. Those who do not learn from history are repeating their defeats. Do not let Satan influence your pride to continue killing innocent people."***

I could see a fortified castle. Jesus said: ***"My people, you have seen many repressive regimes try to force their way of life on others. These conditions have caused many revolutions to overturn such repression. Man will always have an inner desire to be***

free of those enslaving him. It is these circumstances that are causing many of your conflicts. Learn to live in peaceful existence without exploiting your neighbor. By dealing fairly with each other, you will have a better chance of peace."

I could see some pictures of the Declaration of Independence and Constitution documents. Jesus said: ***"My people, when your principles and values are based on My Commandments, your nation has been prosperous with many of My blessings. But when you commit abortions, sins of the flesh, and worship other gods before Me, I will take away your blessings and you will fall in ruin on yourselves. The path your nation is taking is leading you to your demise. So pray, My children, and change your lives, if you expect to continue in My graces."***

I could see some large caves. Jesus said: ***"My people, a time is coming when evil people will despise you for following My ways. You are seeing now how a spiritual battle between good and evil is polarizing parts of your society. Prepare, My people, for a coming religious persecution which you will have to endure for a brief time. Cling to Me and follow My Will and I will protect you from the evil ones who will taunt you. Have faith that one day I will be victorious over all of these evil people. I will chain them in Hell for all of their misdeeds and their refusal to love me."***

I could see some beautiful earthly cities. Jesus said: ***"My people, you think that you can live beautiful lives on the earth with all of your possessions. It is when you are affluent and have everything you want, that you think you do not need Me. You are so confused in loving earthly things for their own sake, yet you are empty inside not realizing you can only be satisfied in Me. You are spiritual beings, so do not let earthly things control you. It is the peace and rest I give your souls through My sacraments that your souls desire most. So, focus your life on your eternal destiny in Heaven and you will realize how keeping your soul clean of sin is your primary care on earth. Come to Me in love and you will be satisfied in giving peace to your spirit."***

I could see some beautiful green mountains and blue seas. Jesus said: ***"My people, I have given you a beautiful world in which to live. I call on you to love one another as I have taught My apostles. I have asked you to endure your neighbors injustices by turning***

the other cheek. I have asked you to walk that extra mile with someone in need. I have taught you to live like the good Samaritan. When you follow My Will of love, everything will be given you. So, follow My plan for your lives, and you will be assured of being with Me in Heaven."

Friday, March 26, 1999:

After Communion, I could see a water wheel bringing up fresh water from a well. Then it slowly disappeared. Jesus said: ***"My people, your fresh water will become more increasingly at risk. Your lakes and rivers are becoming more polluted and despoiled with salt water. With an increasing need for fresh water, people will be fighting over rights to fresh water. Eventually, your governments will so control your water, that it will become rationed. As the time of tribulation arrives, you will need to have the Mark of the Beast to even buy water. This is why I have asked you to store food and water that will become increasingly scarce for My faithful. Pray for My help and I will multiply what you have."***

Later, at Adoration, I could look down a tunnel and someone was looking for books to read in a bookstore. Jesus said: ***"My people, you are curious about many things. If you could list the things that you would like to discover or investigate, you would find many of them would be of an earthly nature. Why are you not more curious about what will happen to you after this life? You should be finding out more about your truths of your faith or looking more in the Scriptures how to imitate My life. By studying My Words and My Revelation in the Scriptures, you will be better prepared to meet Me at your judgment. Come and join Me in Adoration so you can visit Me and grow in the graces I will bestow upon you. In your curiosity seek Me as Mary did and you will choose the better portion that I will not deny you."***

Saturday, March 27, 1999:

Later, after Communion, I could see a picture of the globe of the earth. Jesus said: ***"My people, as you look around the world and consider your recent history, you can see how your wars have been orchestrated by the One World people. Many of these wars have not been in the vital interests of those fighting in them.***

Trumped up dictators and deliberate brutal killings are given as the reasons for your wars. If your industrial defense organization and the arms makers in the world did not have any wars, no money could be made. Just as your abortion doctors collect their blood money, you also have many planned factions in your world collecting their blood money for arms and drugs. Your death culture has even deeper and more insidious roots than you know. It is these people in high places that believe their profits are going unseen. But I see everything and soon My triumph of justice will bring this evil lot to a final end in Hell. Satan and the Antichrist will have their day, but it will all come down in a crashing defeat. Have patience, My faithful, for you will suffer for a short time, before all of these evil people will have to pay for their crimes. Then I will recreate the earth, as all evil will be cleansed. I will raise up an Era of Peace and My faithful will enjoy paradise as you have never seen before."

Later, I could see a young girl next to a sundial in an old picture. Jesus said: ***"My people, many of you have pictures of your relatives who have died. These pictures are a remembrance for you to pray for their souls. If they are in Purgatory, your prayers can help them to leave for Heaven sooner. When you make your prayer intentions, do not limit the scope of your prayers. You can pray for all the souls in Purgatory and multiply your prayers. You can pray for all of your deceased relatives or all those souls in Purgatory who have no one to pray for them. Praying for each other can be a much better gift than any physical present. You have seen the power of prayer on the living in their physical and spiritual problems. Imagine the power of prayer for those who have died. Visiting the grave sites is another way of remembering to pray for your relatives. See that prayer is an expression of your love to Me and to those that you are praying for. Lent is a special time that you should spend more time in prayer."***

Sunday, March 28, 1999: (Passion-Palm Sunday)

After Communion, I could see Jesus' wrapped body laid in the tomb. Jesus said: ***"My people, look upon this transition of your life in death as your pass into Heaven. Without dying to yourself, you cannot be with Me in Heaven. There may be pain at death***

and some hesitation at the unknown, but have no fear because I am at your side. In every painful experience that you go through, there is this painful waiting. Once it is soon over, then you can carry on with your life. So, it is when death is imminent. There is an anxiety of what is to happen. Then after death, you will see a peace of no more testing. For some, you will still have to suffer for a time to purify your soul. Then one day you will be with Me in heavenly paradise. Seek to be faithful in all things, and you will reap your reward with Me. You have seen Me suffer much in My Crucifixion, but it was over in a short time. You then saw My Resurrection in a glorified body. This is My promise to My faithful. If you follow My Will, I will resurrect your bodies as well in a like manner. Then your eyes will be opened to the glory of My eternal reward. Rejoice, as you see My death and Resurrection re-enacted for you once again in Holy Week. Always keep in mind that it was My death that has set you free of your sins. Love Me in return and give thanks to Me for this eternal gift of love."

Monday, March 29, 1999:

After Communion, I could see a pail of cleaning water for cleaning the floor. Jesus said: ***"My people, this Lent has been here for you to get your souls closer to Me by cleansing your sins. By praying more and cleansing your sins in Confession, you can direct your spiritual lives closer to following My Will. You have many earthly distractions that keep you from focusing on Me. You will see when you stop them as a Lenten devotion, it becomes much easier to think of Me and My love. It takes a little courage to do some spiritual spring cleaning of your faults. When you witness My sufferings this week, you will understand more about your purpose here in life to follow Me. Your plans lead to disorder. My plans lead you on your road to Heaven. Your ambitions are to please the body, while My motivation is to direct your spirits to My love. When you see My overwhelming light of love, you will be blinded to any of your earthly desires."***

Later, at the prayer group, I could see many Churches as I moved down the center aisles. Jesus said: ***"My people, many of My faithful are gathering together in the churches this week for Holy Week services. When you gather to commemorate My pas-***

sion and death on the cross, you are all united in My Mystical Body to share in My redemption of your souls. When you have Holy Mass, you are re-enacting My sacrifice in an unbloody manner. This one act of My dying has sent shock waves through the earth and has enabled everyone the opportunity to go to Heaven. I give you your free will to choose to love Me and return your thanks."

I could see a soldier from years past. Jesus said: ***"My people, I call on you to defend your faith by acknowledging My Name and your desire to follow My Commandments. I ask you to be a soldier for Me and proclaim My Word from the rooftops. When you have full belief in Me and realize I am the only life, you should be ready to give your life for Me than deny your faith. I comfort you with My peace and love as you walk on your own road to Calvary."***

I could see many people in a square enjoying a calm life. Jesus said: ***"My people, to live in peace with your neighbor is its own reward. It is when some leaders want to lord it over their own people, that you see these conflicts as in Kosovo. Pray for peace, My children, since war and atrocities will only bring you more grief. Many are searching to protect those being brutally murdered because they see the bodies. I ask you, My people, is there any less reason that you should be seeking to stop the brutal murders of your abortions. Since the media does not show you these bodies, many do not even realize the killing going on. Pray for these mothers to stop killing their babies."***

I could see some TV station trucks and Red Cross vehicles. Jesus said: ***"My people, see how your media is being used by the One World people, to motivate you to supporting war in Yugoslavia. There is an injustice of several thousand people having been killed and many others forced from their homes. But where is the media to show you the atrocities in the womb that are occurring by the millions every year? Money is being made by abortions and by causing wars. This is the very reason you see Kosovo and not the abortion clinics. You have a war zone in your own hospitals where thousands of innocent babies are on the firing line every day. Is there still doubt in your mind that My justice will be raining down on you for these many killings?"***

I could see many smoke clouds from a fire. Jesus said: ***"My people, do not let the One World smoke screen blind your eyes to the many injustices going on right in your own country. As you look upon My suffering, I suffer all of your sins as My Mystical Body suffers. Pray, My children, that you will wake up to your sins and repent of your evil deeds. Change your lives and follow Me if you expect to reach Heaven."***

I could see trees budding and little flowers poking through the ground on a sunny day. Jesus said: ***"My people, as you awake from your winter sleep, come alive to enjoy the signs of spring. As you look on new life springing up, look to your souls to come alive in the grace of My sacraments. It is My rising on Easter that should inspire you to desire a new life with Me in Heaven. Prepare yourselves with Confession and your Lenten devotions, so you can be ready in joy to share Easter morning with Me. My faithful live for the one day that they will be resurrected with Me in Heaven. Be ready, My people, for your reward and your joy will be complete."***

I could see a foggy morning where people in their cars could hardly see to drive. Jesus said: ***"My people, do not let Satan blind you with many earthly distractions. When you go through life only focused on day to day physical life, you are missing many deeper meanings of life seen through the eyes of faith. Take off your spiritual blinders, so you can see life in its entirety. Look for My love in all of My creations, both in nature and in each person. You are a reflection of My love in the image of Myself that I have placed in each individual. Love one another and My peace will be among you. Put aside all of your human aspirations in favor of My heavenly calling."***

Tuesday, March 30, 1999:

After Communion, I could see all of the ruthless dictators over the last century. Jesus said: ***"My people, this age has been tested dearly by dictators with no regard for the value of life. This recent case is just one of many that you have had to deal with. Unfortunately, wars of increasing magnitude resulted in restricting their madness. It is this specter of battle between good and evil that could spread into a larger war. Pray that these battles***

will not spread to other countries. The longer both parties take to resolve their differences, the greater chance for expansion of this war. It will be when more casualties are seen, that your leaders will have to decide on the cost vs. the benefits of further fighting. It is better to refrain from fighting, but Satan is antagonizing the situation with ruthless killing. Continue to pray for a cessation of these hostilities before world war could be threatened."

Later, I could see a large triangle representing the Trinity. There were flashback scenes of Jesus's Baptism, the Transfiguration, and the tongues of fire at Pentecost. Jesus said: ***"My people, My Father, the Holy Spirit, and I are One. There are several references in Scripture when they are acknowledged. I always witnessed to My people that I followed My Father's Will, and because I claimed to know Him, there were many calling Me a blasphemer. In My agony in the Garden, I called on My Father that this cup could pass Me by. But I claimed not My Will, but His be done. Again, on the cross I called on My Father to forgive those who were killing Me. Later, after My Ascension, I sent the Holy Spirit upon My disciples in a wind in the form of tongues of fire. All Three Persons are involved closely with man's salvation. Call on all of Us to help you in life through your prayers. The Trinity is a mystery of faith which is hard for you to understand. You see Us as three separate persons to understand the different attributes of God. Yet, We are all as One Being, calling all of you to love Us. When you make the Sign of the Cross or say the Glory Be, you are invoking Us in your prayer. Prepare yourself to enjoy the coming Triduum of Holy Thursday, Good Friday, and Easter Sunday."***

Wednesday, March 31, 1999:

After Communion, I could see the special markings on the wings of a butterfly. Jesus said: ***"My people, you see the metamorphosis of the caterpillar changing into a flying butterfly. There are many such changes in nature that go through different stages of life as tadpoles change into frogs. I emphasize these stages in life, because you also will be going through a change in your life as well. You grew up from a baby in the womb to later adulthood in the natural life. But it is at death that your body's separation from your soul will bring a new life after death. There is life after*** *the body's death and it could be a beautiful free life of the soul for those who are not bound by sin. For those souls who achieve Heaven you will enjoy a new life of seeing Me in My beatific vision. Later, at the final judgment your soul will be reunited with your glorified body. You will be like the butterfly, only that your radiance will be much greater in your new spiritual life. To live in glory with Me in your own resurrection is what your Easter celebration is all about. You can start this purification process now by pruning out your sins with Confession and enhancing your prayer life. The goal of your soul is to live with Me eternally in Heaven. So, look on death as your freedom to join Me. Seek to keep your souls always pure and ready to receive Me when I come to bring you home."*

Later, at St. Cecilia's tabernacle I could see an old empty wooden casket and the wood was rotted out on the bottom. Jesus said: *"My people, by the time you are being put into your casket, it is too late to change your judgment. Your body soon rots away to nothing and all of your earthly things will mean nothing to you. Focus on the time of your judgment, for you do not know when you are to die. That is why now is the acceptable time to convert your life of sin, before you die. If you keep your soul cleansed with frequent Confession, you will be ready when you die. Your time on this earth is very short. So, spend this brief time working in My service to bring souls to Me. I love My children so much, but you must awaken from your spiritual laziness. Keep focused on Me and I will never let you out of My sight. I am asking you to love Me everyday by showing Me how much you care for Me and care for your neighbor. When you love Me everyday, I will greet you as a friend in Heaven. But if you do not know Me, you will be accursed into the nether world. Come to Me in love and I will never deny you at the Gates of Heaven."*

Index

More Messages from God through John Leary

If you would like to take advantage of more precious words from Jesus and Mary and apply them to your lives, read the first three volumes of messages and visions given to us through John's special gift. Each book contains a full year of daily messages and visions. As Jesus and Mary said in volume IV:

> *Listen to My words of warning, and you will be ready to share in the beauty of the Second Coming.* Jesus 7/4/96
>
> *I will work miracles of conversion on those who read these books with an open mind.* Jesus 9/5/96

Prepare for the Great Tribulation and the Era of Peace

Volume I - ***July 1993 to June 1994,*** ISBN# 1-882972-69-4, 256pp.	$7.95
Volume II - ***July 1994 to June 1995,*** ISBN# 1-882972-72-4, 352pp.	$8.95
Volume III - ***July 1995 to July 10, 1996,*** ISBN# 1-882972-77-5, 384pp.	$8.95
Volume IV - ***July 11, 1996 to Sept. 30, 1996,*** ISBN# 1-882972-91-0, 104pp.	$3.95
Volume V - ***Oct. 1, 1996 to Dec. 31, 1996,*** ISBN# 1-882972-97-X, 120pp.	$3.95
Volume VI - ***Jan. 1, 1997 to Mar. 31, 1997,*** ISBN# 1-57918-002-7, 112pp.	$3.95
Volume VII - ***April 1, 1997 to June 30, 1997,*** ISBN# 1-57918-010-8, 112pp.	$3.95
Volume VIII - ***July 1, 1997 to Sept. 30, 1997,*** ISBN# 1-57918-053-1, 128pp.	$3.95
Volume IX - ***Oct. 1, 1997 to Dec. 31, 1997,*** ISBN# 1-57918-066-3, 168pp.	$3.95
Volume X - ***Jan. 1, 1998 to Mar. 31, 1998,*** ISBN# 1-57918-073-6, 116pp.	$3.95
Volume XI - ***Apr. 1, 1998 to June 30, 1998,*** ISBN# 1-57918-096-5, 128pp.	$3.95
Volume XII - ***July 1, 1998 to Sept. 30, 1998,*** ISBN# 1-57918-105-8, 128pp.	$3.95
Volume XIII - ***Oct. 1, 1998 to Dec. 31, 1998,*** ISBN# 1-57918-113-9, 134pp.	$3.95